Mom and Dad's
Martinis

A Memoir

Jacelyn Cane

Mom and Dad's Martinis
Copyright © 2019 by Jacelyn Cane

All rights reserved. No part of this publication may be reproduced, distributed, or transmitted in any form or by any means, including photocopying, recording, or other electronic or mechanical methods, without the prior written permission of the author, except in the case of brief quotations embodied in critical reviews and certain other non-commercial uses permitted by copyright law.

Tellwell Talent
www.tellwell.ca

ISBN
978-0-2288-0511-3 (Hardcover)
978-0-2288-0510-6 (Paperback)
978-0-2288-0512-0 (eBook)

To my beautiful family,
whom I love more than all the stars in the sky,
more than all the fish in the sea,
more than all the grains of sand on the beach,
more than all the leaves on the trees.

Table of Contents

Introduction vii

Ch 1. Letting Go 1
Ch 2. Take a Powder 11
Ch 3. Covered in Mud 17
Ch 4. He Nailed It 20
Ch 5. Late for the Lord 25
Ch 6. David Willson 29
Ch 7. My Grandmother's Dishes 32
Ch 8. My Father, the Music Man 40
Ch 9. The Canes in Barbados 47
Ch 10. The Gentle Giant 50
Ch 11. The Water Spider 58
Ch 12. The Dark Times I 61
Ch 13. Over the Chair 71
Ch 14. Mom and Vehicles 77
Ch 15. Mom Gets Close 86
Ch 16. The Babysitter 88
Ch 17. The Dark Times II 93
Ch 18. The Parties 108

Ch 19. Dark Times III 127
Ch 20. The Healing 137
Ch 21. The Light 155

Acknowledgements 159
About the Author 161

Introduction

I was rummaging through my memorabilia drawer when I came across the Christmas card Mom sent us in 2014. Usually, she let Hallmark do the talking and would just sign *Love, Mom and Dad*, but this card contained a long message in her almost illegible handwriting, and it was from her alone. She'd addressed it to all of us, including Guinness - that alone was enough to get me crying. As a rule, my mom had no time for dogs - and our lovely Golden was no exception.

When I had originally received the card, I had wept inconsolably, knowing my once vibrant mother was letting go. She had written it from her hospital bed where she had many long hospital stays over several years.

> *Thank you guys for all you have done for me in the last few months. You have been back and forth to the hospital, the condo, helping me, bringing Dad. It is so comforting to know that I can count on you, which has always been the case. I look forward to Christmas with everyone, coming up very soon.*
>
> *All my love,*
> *Mom, Dot, and Granny*

This time, as I read and cried, I decided I would remember my parents by writing a book about them. They were complex, dynamic, sometimes dark, and often humorous people whose stories deserve to be written down. I have included stories that I witnessed and participated in, as well as stories that were told to me by my parents or some of their friends. For the stories that I did not witness, the dialogue has been reconstructed based on the accounts of my parents or others.

1
Letting Go

Dorothy Cane was a spirited woman who approached everything she did with panache.

She was a mother of three, mother-in-law to all our spouses, wife to my father, and grandmother to all our children. She golfed and curled at every opportunity, and her tennis serve was a thing of beauty. An avid volunteer at her church and many other organizations, she was a natural leader.

At age eighty, her health started to fail.

"Mom, your clothes are hanging off of you," I said in her condo one day. "Are you trying to lose weight?" Originally a size sixteen, Mom had never seemed happy with her fuller size. She was now looking closer to a ten.

"No, no. I've just been having a bit of trouble keeping food down lately," said Mom, as she foraged through her jewelry box for earrings to match her outfit.

"Have you been to the doctor?"

"I've got to go, dear," she said. "You know that doctors and I are like oil and water." And with that, she headed to the front hall and out the door, off to serve as a member of the Board of Trustees at her church. She was always going somewhere.

Several months later she called me at about seven in the evening. By this time, she'd drunk four or five martinis - a daily habit. She and my father always had cocktails together before dinner, and dinner was often very late.

"I've lost so much weight, Jackie. I'm down to a size eight," she slurred. "And I'm in pain." She was always so honest when she was drunk. Sometimes I liked her better this way - at least I could find out what she was really thinking and feeling. When she was sober, she played her cards very close to her chest.

"What's going on, Mom?"

"Every time I eat, I'm vomiting, and I have, what's it - diarrhea. Up all night."

"Have you been to the doctor?" I asked again.

"I went. I don't know, was a while ago. He said it was, I was fine."

"Mom, I'm going to call you in the morning and we're going to arrange another appointment for tomorrow. And don't drink anymore tonight."

The next morning when I called, she sounded totally normal. "Mom, it's Jackie. You told me last night that you're down to a size eight, you're throwing up so much. You said you can't sleep."

"I didn't talk to you last night."

"Yes, you did, Mom. You need to get to the doctor today."

"Oh, Jackie. I'll be okay," Mom said. "I'm playing bridge today and having lunch at the club."

I took a breath. She'd always been able to get up early and go, no matter how much she'd had to drink the night before. Most of her friends and colleagues had no idea how many nightly martinis she and Dad drank at home alone.

"How's this?" she said. "I'll call tomorrow and make an appointment for some time soon."

"Mom."

"I've got to go. Love you."

My mother had been one of the few female presidents of the Granite Club – an elite, invitation-only athletic country club in

Toronto. The place was like a second home to her and she wasn't about to let illness get in the way of her bridge game.

Mom eventually shrank down to a size four and spent two years in and out of hospital with colitis and stomach ulcers. Between hospital stays, she kept up with her regular martini intake. Then, Mom had two strokes. She developed congestive heart failure and ischemia of the leg. Her arteries were blocked in her lower legs, especially the left one. Her feet burned, and she could hardly stand the pain. Always fashion conscious, Mom had lived in heels or pointed flats. She now had to succumb to buying orthotic walking shoes, which, for her, was like wearing tugboats on her feet.

The vascular surgeon tried to clean out the arteries in her left leg. Mom found relief for a while, but in no time the arteries clogged again.

My sister and brother and I gathered around Mom's bed to meet the surgeon. "So here are the options," he said. "Mrs. Cane, you can have the surgery; have your left leg amputated from the knee down and be guaranteed to be pain free, but without the movement you're accustomed to. On the other hand, you could forego the surgery and enjoy what time you have left, with movement, but with extreme pain too."

"What about her heart?" my sister Sandy asked. Even though she was the youngest, Sandy was the one my parents relied on the most. She had taken on the role of Mom's medical advocate, so my brother and I let her ask most of the questions.

"Good question," said the surgeon. "The congestive heart failure makes the surgery risky. In the best-case scenario, with congestive heart failure, your mother only has about one year to live. The issue is," he continued matter-of-factly, "does she want to live it pain free?"

"Address my mother, please," Sandy said. My sister was the spitting image of my mother, and they were very close. Duncan and I looked more like my dad - we had his brown eyes and dark hair. Duncan had been given my mom's maiden name as his first name.

Over the next few days, we discussed the options with my mother and called in her minister, The Reverend Dr. Andrew Lawson. He was a large gentleman with distinguished glasses and black hair - Mom talked over the pros and cons with him. They were old friends and Mom trusted his advice. While visiting, Dr. Lawson helped my mother write her own funeral. That was just like my mother to assert control right to the end and beyond.

Finally, my mother decided to go ahead with the amputation. My father was not well enough to be in the waiting room during the surgery, but Sandy, Duncan, and I and two of our spouses surrounded my mother, kissed her, and wished her well. My husband, Ivan, was not able to be there.

"Come on, let's get on with it," Mom said to the nurse. "Chop it off."

We watched as the nurse rolled her away on the stretcher. She disappeared through the operating room doors, not even looking back. We went to the waiting room and sat down.

"I'm going for an Iced Capp," said Sandy. "Anyone want one?"

"No thanks. I'm good," said Duncan.

"Sure, I'll have one," I said. "I'll come with you." My sister and I walked off to the hospital's Tim Horton's and returned with drinks.

"Remember when Mom broke her arm downhill skiing?" I said, sipping my Iced Capp and staring into space. "The funny thing was, she fell while standing at the top of the hill talking to a friend."

"Yeah, she wasn't even skiing," Duncan added. We all laughed nervously.

"And she would spend hours playing golf or tennis or curling," Sandy said.

"Anything to keep moving," I said.

"Code blue. Code blue. Operating room twelve. Code blue." Nurses and doctors from all directions raced past us. I ran up to the nurse's station.

"Is the code blue for Dorothy Cane?" I asked in desperation. "I'm her daughter."

"Yes, it is," said the nurse.

I ran back to the waiting room.

"It's Mom," I announced to everyone. "The code blue is for Mom." My mouth dried up with fear. I paced in one direction while Sandy paced in the other. Duncan and his wife, Liz and Sandy's husband, John sat with their eyes riveted on the floor. A deathly hush fell over the room. Tears streamed down my cheeks as I thought of my mother on that gurney.

"Code blue over. Repeat. Code blue over."

What did that mean? Was Mom okay, or was she dead? Nausea swelled inside my stomach. Time moved slowly.

"Why aren't they coming to talk to us?" Sandy asked. "They said it would be a quick procedure." Silence filled the room.

About an hour later, the surgeon strode into the waiting room.

"Your mother is a lucky woman. She survived the surgery, but just barely." He stood with his legs apart and his hands in the pockets of his hospital gown. He looked so relaxed for someone who had just had my mother's life in his hands. "If I'd come out here thirty minutes ago, it would've been to tell you your mother had died. But she rallied."

"How is she now?" I asked.

"She's very fragile. After recovery, they'll move her to intensive care. You'll have to wait, but you can visit her there. Only two at a time." He discussed her follow-up treatment and was gone.

I entered the darkened ICU wing and immediately smelled the antiseptic in the air. Quietly, I tiptoed past deathly ill patients, each with their own nurse, and searched for bed twenty-two.

All alone, I stood at my mother's bedside. As she slept, I noticed how the sheets folded over one complete leg and only half of the other. From the knee down, my lively mother's leg was gone.

I arrived alone to the ICU again, early the next morning. Mom's heart monitor was beeping steadily and reassuringly, and her nurse sat at a station right at the end of my mother's bed.

"Your mom had a good night," she whispered.

I held my mother's hand. She woke up and smiled at me. She was still groggy, so I sat beside her quietly.

"I'm determined to learn how to move from a bed or a chair into a wheelchair," she said in garbled speech.

"You will, Mom. You will," I said. "All in due time. Let's get you stronger first."

"No, I mean it," she whispered weakly. "I've got to play bridge again."

It wasn't long before Mom was moved from the hospital to a rehabilitation centre. There, the physiotherapist asked her what her goal was.

"I want to go to the Keg next Thursday to celebrate my husband's eighty-fifth birthday." The Keg was one of a popular Canada-wide chain of upscale, family-friendly restaurants, all with the same name. My mom and dad loved their local Keg with its double martinis. Mom was determined to make it for Dad's upcoming birthday.

And she did.

We made sure the Keg had a ramp and reserved an easily accessible table. And, Sandy arranged for a private wheelchair van to pick my mom up at the rehab centre. The day of the party, my sister helped her dress, and, for the first time, my mother didn't care what she looked like. Then, Sandy and a nurse got her into a wheelchair. It was a struggle.

"I'll have a glass of Pinot Grigio," Mom said, as she ordered from the waiter. My mother wasn't drinking martinis anymore. For months before her surgery, she had switched to white wine. "And just a small one." She switched her focus to the family. "It's so good to be together." Just our immediate family and our spouses were present that night. "Charlie, I told you I would make it here, and I did. Happy birthday."

"Thanks, Dot." Dad patted her hand lovingly. "I'm so glad you're here."

Mom ordered a steak and an appetizer. She barely touched her Mushrooms Neptune, so she signalled the waiter. "Can I cancel my steak? I'm not feeling that well."

"Are you okay, Mom?" Sandy asked.

"Oh, I'm fine. I just don't have much of an appetite. Not to worry."

"I think it's fantastic that you're here, Dot," said my brother-in-law, John.

"Oh, you know me, I always do what I say I'm going to do." Mom pushed her appetizer away. "I think I need to head back though."

When the wheelchair van arrived, I escorted her back to the rehab centre. Mom looked so lonely sitting in the back of the van in her wheelchair, as though her future consisted of her all alone in the darkness.

When we reached the centre, I wheeled her to her room and, along with the nurse, helped her get ready for bed.

"Goodnight, Mom," I said, leaning over the bed to kiss her cheek.

She looked up at me, the covers right to her neck. "You know, nothing's ever going to be as easy as it used to be." I could sense the fatigue in her spirit.

My mother's next goal was to celebrate Christmas with all of us. Sandy bought her a beautiful red cape with black fur at the collar and gave it to her as a gift from my father. Then she asked my dad's caregiver to dress him in a red sweater and plaid shirt, so we could take great pictures of my parents together with the entire family.

Everyone gathered at my parents' condo for Christmas dinner. There was a floor to ceiling Christmas tree decorated with silver balls and red ribbons. Pine garland hung across the mantle of the fireplace and smells of cooked turkey drifted from the kitchen.

The grandchildren sat at one table, and my siblings and I sat with Mom and Dad and our spouses at another.

"Mom, I have to tell you how much you've inspired me these past few months," my sister-in-law, Liz said. "Your determination has been incredible."

"That's nice, Liz," said Mom. "I just did what I had to do."

My mom wanted to serve the English trifle for dessert, something she hadn't done in years. "It means so much to me to be with all of you." She made sure that everyone heard her, including the grandchildren at the other table.

After dinner, we all kissed her and told her how much we loved her. That probably wasn't a good idea because the next day Mom came down with the flu. When I dropped in to visit her at the rehab centre, she was as white as her bed sheets.

"Mom, that's a terrible cough." I touched her forehead. "And I'm sure you've got a fever. I'll get the doctor." By the following day, my mother had pneumonia. She was immediately sent back to the hospital.

"I don't want to be here," she cried from her hospital bed. "I'm tired – tired of living. I've tried so hard, but I'm always getting sick. Life is so difficult now. It's never going to get better."

I felt a lump in my throat and choked back tears. It was hard to hear that my mother had had enough.

Again, my siblings and I gathered around her - this time to say good-bye. Sandy wheeled my father in.

"Good-bye, Charlie," whispered Mom as loudly as she could. "I love you." She reached out a hand to touch his.

"I love you, too, Dot. Everything's gonna be okay." Dad tapped her hand in his loving way. He didn't totally understand the significance of the visit. But Bailey, his caregiver, did. She was a tiny woman who was strong enough to manage my father's increasingly ornery behaviour and gentle enough to love us all. She had looked after my mother and father for many years and was like a member of the family. She stood in the corner of my mom's hospital room sobbing.

Reverend Lawson came for one last visit, too. My mom stopped eating. She wouldn't even take an ice chip. She had decided it was time to die and that was that. The palliative care team at the hospital honoured her wishes. My siblings and I and our spouses sat around and waited.

At one point, in a state of delirium, my mother sat up in her bed and yelled out, "I want to stand up." We helped her lie back down.

Later, she started ripping off her hospital gown. "I don't want this. I don't want this anymore."

"Mom, you've got to keep your gown on," Sandy said, as we tried desperately to keep her clothes on.

We started taking shifts so that someone was always with her. My sister stayed overnight on the first night. When my eldest daughter, Eliana, arrived to join me for my shift, the next night, Mom's eyes were wide open, looking like robin-egg-blue marbles, but she was asleep.

"That sometimes happens when people are near death," the nurse explained tenderly. Eliana and I sat watching my mother and holding her hands.

"Eli," I whispered around five o'clock that evening. "Granny's not breathing. She's gone."

"What do we do?" asked Eliana. She stood up and ran out into the hall. "Someone come please. My grandmother is dead. Someone. She's dead."

A nurse came and told us she would bring in the medical examiner.

I kissed my mom and closed her eyelids. I gently stroked her cheeks. At that moment, I felt relief and shock. I was filled with a sense of disbelief as though I was watching this scene unfold from above. This was the moment I had known was coming for some time now. Where was the script I was supposed to follow, I wondered. Eliana and I sat there in silence.

Mom's funeral was just as she had wanted it to be. It included her chosen hymns: "O Master, Let Me Walk with Thee," "Will Your Anchor Hold," and "I See the Love of God in Every River." My brother gave the eulogy.

"There was the time Mom bought a used Mercedes Benz and thought she had such a classy car," Duncan said. "The thing didn't even make it home before it broke down."

His eulogy was full of humour, just the way my mother would have liked it. Her eldest grandson, Robbie, read from the Bible. And Reverend Lawson gave a meditation about my mother that showed how well he knew her and admired her. "I remember golfing with Dorothy, Robbie, and his dad John Cowan," said Reverend Lawson. "Not being much of a golfer, I wasn't sure if knee socks with shorts were part of the proper attire, but I wore them anyways because I knew Dorothy wouldn't mind what I had on." And later, he added, "Dorothy loved this church and wasn't afraid to challenge me after a meeting if she thought our decisions were taking us in the wrong direction. She was a principled woman."

Hundreds of people who had known her and loved her gathered to say good-bye. Following the funeral, there was a reception at the Granite Club with a light lunch and, of course, an open bar.

2

Take a Powder

May, 1973

Mom and Dad sipped their martinis from their usual lowball glasses. They liked their martinis dry: straight gin on the rocks with a dab of vermouth and a hint of water. It was a frequent ritual to wet their whistles while getting ready for one of their many social engagements.

This night was a particularly important occasion. It was the night of the inauguration ball.

"Charlie, your white dinner jacket and black pants are back from the cleaners. They're lying on the bed." Mom's Grace Kelly blonde hair shone, and she smiled her dazzling smile, as she applied her light-pink lipstick. I was nineteen and, even though it was Saturday, I was home for the evening. Both of my siblings had gone out. Dad was shaving in the bathroom.

I watched from my parents' bedroom door as Mom touched up her rouge and stroked on her lilac eyeshadow. She leaned towards the mirror, widening her eyes, as she brushed her mascara on ever so carefully. Admiring herself, she tossed her curls back and put on her pearl earrings and necklace. Then she slipped into her full-length mauve organza gown with its satin sash and frill around the neck. She put on her beaded heels and grabbed the matching clutch purse.

"Dot, can you help me with this?" Dad needed Mom's help to get the bow just right under his double chin. Leaving the button undone on his white jacket, he looked in the mirror, combed his thinning black hair, put on his glasses, and tucked his acceptance speech into his breast pocket.

"What do you get up to at the Gyro Club anyway?" I asked as I followed them down the hall towards the front door.

"It's a very special club for businessmen. It's not easy to get into … and it's been around for decades," said Dad.

"It's a vital place for Dad to meet new clients. How do you think he got to be top salesman at Canada Life?" Mom asked, adding, "I made you some stew, Jackie. It's on the stove."

Dad grabbed his car keys. "The club's mission statement is easy to remember - three words: 'power, poise, and purpose.'"

"It's a big deal for Dad to be chosen as president," said Mom, as I draped her mink stole around her shoulders.

"Well, you both look spectacular. Have a wonderful time. Good luck." I watched them drive off and closed the door behind me.

"The room was beautiful," Mom told me the next day. "Gold curtains, crystal chandeliers, and mahogany walls and floor. The tables were all set with white linen tablecloths and pink and red roses as centrepieces."

She told me Dad gave his acceptance speech and was honoured with a presidential pin. Then the two of them socialized, drank, and danced through the night - they were good at all three. The band played big-band jazz: Benny Goodman, Tommy Dorsey, Glenn Miller, and more. The night wound down and people started leaving.

"Charlie, let's go." Mom grabbed her purse.

Dad was busy finishing his last drink and chatting with well-wishers. "Why don't you get your mink at the coat check? I'll be right behind you."

Mom and Dad's Martinis

Mom headed out to the car, passing by the large shallow pool with red tulips and yellow daffodils all around the edges. She turned back to see if Dad was coming.

"There you are. Usually, I'm the last one to leave." Walking backwards as she spoke, she tripped over the flowers. Arms flailing, she stumbled back. Mink stole, mauve organza, beaded purse and all, she buckled backwards into the pool, dragging tulips and daffodils with her. She lay there, legs and arms splayed. Her curls were no longer. Her mink was drenched.

"Dot! What the hell are you doing?" Dad yelled. "Your mink is ruined!"

Mom's mascara ran down her cheeks. "Well, I didn't do it on purpose - and would you mind asking me if I'm okay?"

"Jesus Christ, Dot! I knew you'd had too much to drink." Dad stepped over the flowers and knelt down by my mom.

"I didn't drink any more than you did. Just get me out of here, for Christ's sake."

He looked around. "Here, pass me your mink before it drowns you." He grabbed the soaked stole and placed it on the cement. "Give me your hand. Come on, Dot. Let me get you out of there before other people see you."

Guests began to crowd around.

"Dot, what happened?" asked Harry Brown.

"You must be freezing. I'll get you some tablecloths," said his wife, Nan.

"Charlie, get her out of there," another woman demanded.

"Does anyone have a camera?" Harry inquired. A small crowd had gathered and people were laughing.

"No photos," said Dad. "It's bad enough that she's in there. We don't need to remember it."

"I'd like a picture to send out at Christmas, actually," said my mother, as he helped her to stand.

"Oh, come on, Charlie. It's funny. This is a quintessential Dot move," said another guest.

"You've got that right," Dad admitted, as he started to laugh. "Come on, Dot, get out of there."

"Let me just get my purse. Where is it?"

The purse had spilled its contents. She fished for lipstick, powder, cigarettes, and house keys as bits of daffodils and tulips floated by.

Dad finally managed to get her out, dripping organza clinging to her legs. Water squished out of her shoes, so she shuffled along in her nylons, carrying her shoes and her purse. My father wrapped her in a tablecloth and helped her slide into the car. He threw the soaked mink, also wrapped in linen, in the backseat.

My bedroom was right beside the front door. In the middle of the night, I heard knocking on the glass. "Jackie, wake up." My mother's voice. "I fell in a pool and lost my house keys. Jackie, honey, open the door."

I dragged myself out of bed and shuffled to the front hall. Rubbing the sleep out of my eyes, I unlocked the door and stepped back so my parents could enter. Mom was wrapped up like a mummy, and her wet hair was matted around her face. Dad's white dinner jacket had black blotches all over it, and he was carrying what looked like a wet lump of laundry.

"That's right, your mother fell in the pool. Can you lay her mink out in your bathtub to dry?" Dad handed me the fur. "We'll tell you the details in the morning. Let's just say the 'poise' part of the mission statement was a bust."

* * *

May, 1974

When the inaugural ball rolled around the next year, Dad's role, as the incumbent, was to introduce the new president and accept the post of past president. On the afternoon of the grand occasion, Mom assured herself there would be so slip-ups that night. She walked into the closet she and Dad shared and began to lay out their clothes for the evening. Picking up the black silk and satin gown she'd bought for the event, she laid it down on the bed and admired it. She grabbed the black satin purse and shoes and put them on the bed, too.

Mom walked back into the closet to get Dad's white dinner jacket and black pants. No plastic wrap. "Christ." She'd forgotten to take them to the cleaners after last year. "God Almighty, look at all those black smudges on his jacket." He was going to kill her. Mom stared in horror at the jacket for a long moment. Then she had an idea. She hustled into the bathroom, grabbed the talcum powder and a face cloth, and, with a little sprinkle here and there, began to coat the black spots. Sprinkle, dab, sprinkle. "Not bad." She rubbed it in a bit more. Sprinkle, dab, sprinkle.

When Dad came home, he poured the martinis and they got dressed. Mom looked stunning in her black gown and Dad looked classy in his white jacket - you couldn't see the marks. Dad didn't notice a thing. Mom was wearing a new mink coat - her stole had never recovered. Off they went to the ball.

After the Chicken Kiev, Dad, at the head table, gave a crowd-pleasing speech that included a joke about a wet mink. Then the dancing began - the same big band music with a bit more Frank Sinatra and Louis Armstrong thrown in for variety.

"Come on, Dot, let's dance." Dad took Mom's hand and together they sashayed around the dance floor. Dad drew Mom in and then twirled her out - in, out, in, out. "Dot, what are those white marks on your dress?"

"Oh, it's nothing, dear - just some powder from my compact." Mom tried to wipe off the telltale white, but with little success.

As they switched dance partners time and time again, Dad found he was leaving white patches on every woman's dress.

"Charlie, what happened to your dinner jacket," asked Mrs. Hunter, a large-bosomed woman with blue-grey hair swirled up in a bun. "Your jacket, Charlie - it's covered in black marks."

Her own dark-red dress had two white blotches, one on the centre of each of her breasts.

Dad went to the washroom and, looking in the mirror, saw that his dinner jacket was a wreck - filthy with black blots.

On the way home, Mom confessed what she'd done.

"Geez, Dot, it's your job to take care of the home front. What were you thinking?"

"That's not all I do, and you know it." Mom said. "I'm running the lottery for the art gallery. That's an incredible amount of work. I'm still volunteering at the church."

"Yeah, yeah, I know, but I'm the breadwinner, and I count on you to keep things going at home."

"And I do. Breakfast and dinner are on the table for you and the kids every night."

"I know, I know. But you pulled a fast one on me tonight." Dad turned the corner.

"Yeah, but, you've got to admit it was kind of funny."

As always, Dad soon calmed down and was able to see the humour in the situation. He even wanted to know how Mom put the talcum powder on his jacket. That was the way my parents rolled.

3

Covered in Mud

In October of 1950, Dad met Mom for the first time in a local Kingston, Ontario drug store. "Are you Dorothy Duncan?" he asked, as he approached her at the drug store's soda fountain. "I'm Charlie Cane. He pointed to his letterman jacket. "I'm from U of T -Chemical Engineering."

Mom was dressed in her soft-blue poodle skirt and white cardigan sweater. She fixed the blue scarf tied around her neck. "How did you know my name?" she asked, as she sized him up. He looked about six foot four, and was wearing grey flannels and a dark-blue pullover with a white shirt and a thin maroon tie. His short black hair was parted at the side and combed neatly back. Dad had heard from friends that Mom would be at the drug store that afternoon and sought her out. He was clearly trying to make a good impression.

"Oh, I saw your photo on the UC Follies flyer. You're directing the talent show at U of T this year, aren't you?" Dad leaned up against the counter.

"Yes, I am."

"Well, I figured you're here in Kingston to go to the Queen's - U of T homecoming game.

She nodded.

"I wondered if you'd like to go to the Queen's dance with me tonight."

Shifting on her red vinyl stool, my mother sipped her Coke float. "Why don't you meet me here at five o'clock after the game, and I'll give you my answer then."

Dad strolled out over the black and white linoleum tiles thrilled he had a chance for the date he had hoped for.

"Now, there goes a tall drink of water," said one of my mom's pals, eyeballing my father as he left.

My dad made his way to the Queen's football stadium to meet his friends for the game.

"Charlie, did you bring a mickey?" one of Dad's buddies asked, as they all found some seats together in the bleachers.

"Rye." My dad tapped his breast pocket. "You brought something, too, right?" Dad addressed the four fellows sitting alongside of him.

"Yeah, I've got some rum," said Dad's friend, John Beatty.

"Me, too," said a chubby student next to John.

"I've got scotch," the third man claimed.

"Gin for me," added the last one in the group.

"Hey, U of T's winning," said John.

"Touchdown!" My father cheered, as he leapt in the air. He took a swig of his rye to celebrate.

"We scored again," Dad yelled gleefully, bouncing up and down. With every jump, he took another nip from his mickey.

"We won!" My dad cheered. As he sprang to his feet, he tripped and fell onto the bleachers. His mickey broke, making Dad reek of alcohol. He managed to clean up all of the glass without a scratch, but, nevertheless, he was covered in rye.

By the end of the game, when he joined in the age-old tradition of running out on to the field to climb up on the goalposts, Dad was pretty drunk. He lost his balance and fell in the mud. Before he could get to his feet, he was stepped on by a few members of the

Queen's marching band. His letterman jacket and grey flannels were covered in mud.

And so, muddy, inebriated, and stinking of booze, my father returned to meet Mom after the game. He swaggered into the drug store, leaving muddy footprints in his wake, as he made his way across the linoleum floor. Patti Page's version of "Tennessee Waltz" was playing on the juke box.

"Hi, Dorothy Duncan. Sorry, I'm a bit of a mess. I'm hoping you'll go with me to the dance tonight."

"No thanks," she said in disgust, as she eyed him up and down.

"You're sure? I'll get cleaned up and everything."

"I said, 'No.' Now excuse me." Mom stood up, walked passed Dad and out of the drug store.

Dad stood there covered in mud looking like a lost puppy.

4

He Nailed It

Back in Toronto, Dad, cleaned up this time, asked Mom out again. She agreed to go with him to the University of Toronto's varsity dance the following Saturday.

Mom wore a calf-length dark-green taffeta dress with a cinched waist. Thanks to the crinoline, the skirt was so full it could stand up on its own. Dad dressed in a navy-blue suit with wide lapels and shoulders and a matching blue bowtie - no mickey in his pocket that night. Together they danced to dreamy music, like Nat King Cole's "Mona Lisa" and the Ames Brothers' "Sentimental Me."

"You're quite the dancer, Dot. Can I call you Dot?" asked my dad.

"Of course." She smiled at him. "I'm not calling you Charles, am I?" Together, they swayed around the dance floor. Mary Coxwell swung past them in the arms of a heavy-set boy in a varsity sweater, followed by Sue Conway and her boyfriend, Ed. Mom looked over Dad's shoulder at her two best friends and smiled.

Later that Saturday night, the three girls, with curlers in their hair, sat cross-legged on my mother's bed. They always curled their hair for church on Sundays, regardless of what had happened on Saturday nights.

"Did you see that fellow with Eve?" Mary stretched out on her side in her checkered jammies. "Wasn't he dreamy?" She raised her eyes to the ceiling.

"And, what about Cassie's new boyfriend?" said Sue. "I wouldn't mind taking a walk with him." The three of them giggled.

"Never mind all that," said Mom. "I've met the man I want to spend the rest of my life with." She threw her arms up in the air. Mary hugged her while Sue bounced on the bed.

Dad was equally taken with Mom. Their university classes ended at the same time at opposite ends of the U of T campus, so he would bolt across the university grounds on his lanky legs, just to meet Mom.

"Can I ... carry your books, Dot?" he asked one day bent over and out of breath. "And ... can I ... take you for coffee?"

"Why thanks, Charlie. I'd love to," Mom handed her books to my dog-tired dad. From that day forward, they became an item. Dad spent so much time with Mom he became known as "The Shadow" - a nickname that stuck throughout their married life.

* * *

Mom and Dad had been dating for about a year when Dad graduated and found a job that required him to relocate to Montreal. The separation was difficult for both of them. Dad was spending a fortune on phone calls to Mom every night, and Mom felt an aching lump of loneliness in her stomach. In time, he started coming back to Toronto to see her every weekend. It wasn't long before they became engaged and made plans for a wedding at Timothy Eaton Memorial Church in Toronto's Forest Hill where Mom had been a member of the congregation since she was a child.

It was a crisp fall day, and, as Mom stood shivering in her white satin and lace gown on the front steps of the church, Mary handed her the flowing bouquet of white roses. Dad and his six attendants wore tails. Mom had five bridesmaids and a flower girl who all wore full-length olive-green velvet and satin dresses and velvet pill box hats. My parents wed on October 13th, 1951.

It was a dry reception - not because my grandfather didn't drink, but because he didn't want to spend money on the bar. It was held in the Imperial Room at the Royal York Hotel in Toronto. One hundred and fifty guests dined and danced in the magnificent dining room with its full-length windows, elaborate ceiling, beautiful wooden dance floor, and stage for the band.

The reception was suddenly interrupted when Princess Elizabeth arrived at the hotel with full security detail.

"Dot, Princess Elizabeth is here. She's pulling up at the front door now. Let's go."

"Princess Elizabeth, here? I've got to see this!" Mom stopped dancing with her father and, along with dozens of wedding guests, ran out of the Imperial Room to catch a glimpse. Out by the front door, she spotted the princess's car. "Hoist me up." Mom yanked her wedding dress up around her hips and, with the help of her friends, dragged herself up onto one of the enormous flowerpots at the front door of the hotel. "Here she comes. She's coming! Princess Elizabeth, over here! Hello, Princess Elizabeth. It's my wedding day." My mother stood in the flowerpot, with her white satin shoes in the soil, delighted to see the princess up close. Dad was standing behind Mom, silently enjoying her kooky spirit.

* * *

After their honeymoon in the Bahamas, my parents moved into a two-bedroom apartment at Yonge and Sheppard in Toronto. The neighbourhood was much quieter and quite a distance away from where either of my parents had grown up. My mother's cooking agreed with my dad so much that he gained fifty pounds in their first year of marriage. Eighteen months after their wedding, my brother Duncan was born. Parenthood didn't stop Mom and Dad from having the odd party. In fact, the landlord asked them to stop entertaining because of all the noise. My dad argued with him, but eventually agreed to curtail the partying.

My parents did decide to have a party one Sunday afternoon to celebrate my brother's first birthday though. Mom and Dad invited both sets of grandparents, and great-grandparents, along with aunts and uncles, to drop in for a piece of cake. Harmless enough, or so they thought.

It was raining, and all their guests' galoshes were lined up outside the apartment. Inside, my grandfather was telling his famous corny jokes. "Why shouldn't you write with a broken pencil?" he asked, his voice booming from the depths of his rotund frame. "Because it's pointless. Get it?" Everyone howled with laughter just because Grandpa got such a kick out of himself. "Here's another one: 'What's a golf club's favourite type of music?'"

"I don't know, Dad," said my mother.

"Why, swing of course!" My grandfather gave a loud belly laugh. Everyone roared.

Shortly after, Dad took out his ukulele. He was a virtuoso - even back then. Together they sang "All of Me," "I've Got My Love to Keep Me Warm," and "Happy Days Are Here Again." They finished with a rousing round of "Happy Birthday" for my brother. There was nothing quiet about their singing.

The landlord, Mr. Perkins, heard the ruckus. He stuck his thumbs in the straps of his overalls. *Those low-lifes.* Down he went to his workroom, grabbed some tools, and returned to the hallway outside my parents' apartment. With great determination, he meticulously drove a nail or two through the inner sole of every boot, until all the rubbers were nailed to the floor.

Eventually the music died down, and it came time for the relatives to go home. My grandmother, attempted to slip into her boot. "Gracious, me…." She floundered and fell over, as her stylish blue pancake hat slid off her head.

My great-grandmother tried to put on her galoshes. She shrieked and lurched forward, bringing my great uncle down with her.

"Oh, mother, I'm so sorry!" Uncle Donald said, as he rolled off his mother, stood up and tripped over a great aunt whose feet were caught in her nailed-down rubbers.

My parents watched helplessly as family members tumbled on top of each other, landing in a heap.

"Here, give me your hand," said my mother. With her baby son in one arm, she tried to help aunts and uncles up with the other. My father managed to lift my great-grandmother up off the ground relatively unscathed.

"That jerk nailed everything to the floor," said Dad. He darted into the apartment, came out with a hammer and frantically dislodged the nails. Initially, my parents were embarrassed by this incident. Soon, however, they laughed, and the tale went into the canon of classic Cane stories.

5

Late for the Lord

Years passed, and my parents had three children: my brother, then me, followed by my sister. My parents were big on church, but not on religion – at least, I didn't think so when I was young. Even though we lived in the suburbs, and my parents would party until four in the morning most Saturday nights, we continued to drive forty-five minutes to Timothy Eaton in Forest Hill for the earliest Sunday morning service.

On Sunday mornings, my parents rolled out of bed hungover.

"Jesus Christ. Get moving kids," my Dad yelled one typical Sunday morning. "No time for breakfast. We have to be out of here in half an hour." He stood in an usher's getup of tails and pain-striped pants, gulping some Alka-Seltzer.

"Dad's wearing his penguin suit again," my brother said.

My mother taught Sunday school each week, but first, her job was to make sure we three kids looked perfect in thirty minutes.

"Duncan, your blazer, shirt, tie, grey flannels, and oxfords are on your chair. And for God's sake, make sure you wear clean underwear."

My sister and I were more labour intensive; as girls, we had to match. We wore identical dresses, hats, coats, fancy ankle socks, and patent leather shoes. I always felt like I was getting ready for a big show. My mother dressed herself last in about five minutes. She usually left the house with mascara from the night before smudged under her eyes.

The five of us piled into my father's Chrysler and he high tailed it across the 401, down Avenue Road and through the back streets of Forest Hill. "Jesus Christ, we're hitting every red light," he said in exasperation. "We're never going to get there on time."

As usual, there was no parking left when we arrived.

"Aw, for Christ's sake, where am I going to put this car?" Dad always parked legally. If my Mom had been driving, it would've been a different story.

"Get out. Everybody out. I'll find parking and be right in." We all tumbled out and scrambled into church - stopping for just a second at the grand oak doors to straighten ties, pull up socks, and tidy dresses and hats.

I loved our church with its high cathedral ceilings and its stained-glass window of Jesus holding the light of the world. Solid oak beams reached to the ceiling, embracing the majestic stone walls. The pews were built of the same dark wood. The organist began playing a grand prelude followed by the processional hymn "All Things Bright and Beautiful." The choir processed down the centre aisle in their gowns, while the entire congregation sang along. The choral conductor followed the choir and then came the ministers in their black robes and coloured stoles. The senior minister entered last and climbed several stairs to the intricately carved pulpit from where he would preach.

When my dad finished with his ushering duties, he joined us and my grandparents in the family pew. Dad leaned over to me and whispered, "Jackie, look at that ceiling. How many tiles do you think there are up there?" Anything to keep his mind off the church service. Meanwhile, the other adults in the family stared ahead, listening to the Bible readings, while Sandy and Duncan flipped through the bulletin for entertainment.

Mom and Dad's Martinis

Later, while listening to my mother teach my Sunday school class about the Holy Trinity, I noticed she was wearing a brown high heel on her left foot and a blue one on her right. She dealt with the error by pointing it out to people, as she chatted after church. That was my mother. She had no shame. She was just happy our family had made it to the service.

On the ride home, I was the one with the questions. I thought a lot about God when I was young. "Mom, how can God be the Father, Son, *and* the Holy Ghost?"

"Dear, it's not polite to talk about religion after church," my mother answered.

I fiddled with the buckle on my purse. "Dad, how could Jesus rise up from the dead?"

"Christ Almighty, Jackie. Can't you see I'm concentrating on my driving?"

We drove along Yonge Street, and then Dad pulled into Hall's Dairy where they made the best milkshakes in town - a sure sign our parents were hungover. We walked in and sat at a table. Dad went up to the counter in his tails. "Five large chocolate shakes please." Dad paid for the shakes and walked over to our table, carrying a tray with five silver canisters. As he sipped his milkshake, he said, "Geez, if I knew I'd be this thirsty today, I would have had more to drink last night."

When my siblings and I grew up, we stopped going to church or attended different ones. My parents, however, continued to attend Timothy Eaton faithfully until their failing health made that impossible.

Mom, in particular, was a committed church volunteer. Upon her retirement at Timothy Eaton, the church secretary sent my mother a thank-you note. "TEMC is a much better institution because of your stewardship. The list of committees you served on seems endless: Stewardship, Special Events, Property (Chair), Trustees, Congregational Board and Elder, Lawson Group and Sanctuary Guild - and not just one at a time but all, all of the time."

When I read this note, I understood why my mother was so often either not at home or on the phone.

    The first time my sister and I attended Timothy Eaton together after our parents' deaths, the church felt cavernous. It echoed with memories. When I cried through the processional hymn, my sister placed her hand on top of mine. Now we attend Timothy Eaton occasionally. I find it feels sad to be there - my parents are woven into the fabric of that congregation. Nevertheless, I also feel warmed by the many wonderful childhood memories I have of that church.

6

David Willson

My mother's ancestors were especially interesting on my grandmother's side - at least I thought so. Mom was never too impressed with her own family history. Her grandfather, seven generations back, was David Willson, born in 1778. Willson was the son of Presbyterian linen merchants who had come from Antrim in Northern Ireland to New York State in the early 1700s. Not long after, they moved north to Hope (now called Sharon) in York County, Upper Canada. It was there that Willson married a Quaker and began following her religious traditions. He missed the music of his religious upbringing, however, and so he began his own sect, known as the Children of Peace. Music was a huge part of sect's tradition.

Willson spearheaded the building of the Sharon Temple, based on the biblical description of Solomon's Temple. Constructed between 1825 and 1831, the building still stands today as a National Historic Site. Designed around a concept of equality, all windows and other parts of the structure are equal distance from each other; all pews face the centre where the minister speaks. Willson also commissioned the first organ to be constructed in Upper Canada - the Children of Peace developed the first civilian band in the country. Because of the temple's wonderful acoustics, many concerts were held there for decades, until wear and tear began to take its toll on the historical structure.

The sect lived as a cooperative with a land-sharing system. Members of the Children of Peace sold their wheat according to their needs, rather than the highest amount the market would bear. With Willson at the helm, the sect founded the first homeless shelter in Upper Canada and began the province's first credit union.

Willson was also an important political reformer, working closely with William Lyon Mackenzie, who became the first mayor of Toronto in 1834. Along with Mackenzie, Willson spoke out against the autocratic Family Compact - merchants, Anglican clergymen, and members of government who controlled most of the land in Upper Canada.

All of this was too much for my mother. She was a traditionalist in many ways and a Tory through and through. She certainly didn't want to have anything to do with cooperatives and rebellions. Once, I travelled with my husband and children to visit the Sharon Temple; we were so excited to see the interior and learn about the history. When I told my mother about the visit, she said, "Why are you spending time in a temple?" It was as though we had joined a cult.

I doubt Willson would have seen it that way. Having come from the United States, and emboldened by that country's revolutionary spirit, he was very wary of British conformity. Within a reform movement of unhappy farmers and tradesman, he inspired the Children of Peace and other settlers to fight for democracy. With Willson's support, William Lyon Mackenzie, having finished serving as mayor of Toronto, attempted to overthrow the provincial government in the Upper Canada Rebellion of 1837. Willson's sons fought in the unsuccessful rebellion and were jailed for months afterwards.

While Willson never trained as a minister or had a university education, he served as preacher and theologian for the Children of Peace and wrote many hymns until his death in 1866. After his death, without him as their leader, the Children of Peace soon faded out.

As a rebel myself, I have always admired Willson. I also relate to his love of music and feel it has a real place in my family. I believe that Willson's spirit is alive in my immediate family and me today.

7

My Grandmother's Dishes

My mom grew up on Tarlton Road in Forest Hill, Toronto. For many years, she lived a charmed childhood. Every day, my mother swallowed her molasses and cod liver oil and strolled to school with her neighbours and lifelong best friends, Mary and Sue. Off they went, down Tarlton West, onto Chaplin Crescent, through the park, over the railroad tracks and on to Forest Hill Jr. School. It was a long walk for little girls - and they came home for lunch every day.

In the evenings, after supper, Mom would bounce outside to play with the neighbourhood kids - hide and seek, cowboys and Indians, and red rover. Along with her girlfriends, my mother tried to master "double Dutch" skipping and threw a rubber ball against the house singing "Ordinary Moving". On the lawn, the girls muddled through cartwheels, back bends, somersaults, and even some Russian dancing.

On rainy days, Mom and her girlfriends gathered in her basement to dress up in outrageous costumes - hats, high heels, and jewellery. Thanks to my grandmother, everything was packed in an old trunk and a dress up closet. One Sunday night, together in their dresses and high heels, my mother and her girlfriends paraded around to music played on a wind-up Victrola - "String of Pearls," "Perfidia," and more. And while they played, smells of my grandmother's roast-beef wafted to the basement.

"Dorothy," my grandmother called down.

"Yes, Mommy."

"It's time for dinner. The girls need to go home now."

"Already?"

"Yes, dear. You'll see them after dinner."

Every Sunday night, they had a scrumptious roast-beef dinner in the dining room with the family, including Aunt Geraldine, my grandmother's sister.

"This plate is for you, Dorothy," said Mom's mother, as she scooped some roasted potatoes onto my mom's plate. On Sunday nights, they always used Grandma Duncan's good china – made in France with two exquisite blue and green birds sitting on branches. "Hold it carefully, dear." Mom's mother loved that china, and so my mom loved it, too. They always had wonderful conversations in the dining room and Mom looked forward to those meals. Her mom was a great hostess and my mother became one, too.

Soon, my mother and her closest girlfriends - Mary, Sue, and Helen - were labeled "the Tarlton Road Gang." Eglinton Avenue was just beginning to be a place to hang out - and the soda fountain at Kresge's discount store was a favourite destination.

"Let's go to Kresge's for a cherry Coke," my mom said one afternoon.

"I'm gonna get a banana split," Helen added, fixing the large bow in her curly hair. "They're the best in town."

Mom and her friends sat on bar stools at Kresge's long counter and finished their treats. "I know, let's head over to 'B and W's' for some red licorice," Mary said, pulling her socks up from her saddle shoes.

"I want to buy some candy cigarettes and bubble gum," Sue said.

"Let's do that later. The Eglinton Theatre's open," said Mom. "Let's go to the matinee. Have you all got a quarter?" She was always the one organizing things.

In the summers, my mother and her closest girlfriends attended Camp Glen Bernard, on Lake Bernard, in Sundridge, Ontario. She loved the musicals they put on each summer, and the singsongs, canoeing, swimming, and more. Most of all, she valued the camaraderie. Years later, Mom found out that my dad's relatives had attended the same summer camp. My sister and I carried on the tradition by working there, and my niece attended both as a camper and a counsellor for years.

As Mom got a bit older, she and her pals began suntanning with baby oil and iodine. My mother continued her career of being in charge when she ran for school president at Forest Hill Collegiate. She used Sammy Kaye's "Daddy" - a song that later turned out to be one of my dad's all-time favourites - as the tune for her campaign theme song.

Hey students, you want a president who will see you through?
Then students, Duncan's the one for you.
She'll be a great sensation.
She'll be your inspiration.
Hey students, Duncan's the one for you.

Of course, she won and had a very successful year. Friday night dances were better than ever. Mom also won the Tamblyn Award that year - a citywide contest for the grade thirteen student showing the best academic promise and leadership skills.

* * *

Unfortunately, Mom's childhood wasn't all bliss. Her mother became ill the year Mom turned twelve. My grandmother continued to carry out her motherly duties throughout her sickness, still making lunch for my mom and her sister every day.

One day at lunch, Mom and her sister Ruth raced each other home from school and ran in the front door giggling. "Beat you," said Ruth.

"Yeah, well you're four years older," said Mom. The girls stopped in their tracks at the sight of their mother leaning against the counter, barely able to stand up.

"Girls," she called breathlessly. "Come ... and ... eat."

The girls quietly ate their lunch, with every bite of their sandwiches and slurp of their soups breaking the silence. "Mom, Mrs. Thomas said she liked my story," my mother said, trying to make conversation.

"That's ... nice ... dear," whispered her mother, as she sat bent over the kitchen table.

My mother and her sister finished up quickly. "Thanks, Mom. We love you," my mother said, kissing her mom on the cheek.

"I've got to go ... back ... to bed," Grandmother Duncan said, struggling to get the words out. And then, she crawled up the stairs. Mom watched helplessly as the centre of her universe faded away.

One February afternoon, she returned home to find her father sitting at the kitchen table. Her mother was gone. Mom never knew the exact cause. Perhaps it was asthma? Or maybe breast cancer? As was often the custom in those days, my grandmother's body was embalmed and laid out on the family's living room couch for viewing. My mother and her sister were forced to sit vigil for days while people dropped by. Mom tried not to look at her mother's pale, waxy body. It was dressed in the blue suit she so often wore to church on Sundays.

"Now, girls, remember - no tears," said Mom's father. "I won't have it, you hear? Smile, Dorothy. Here come the Coxwells with Mary. Make conversation."

"Hello, George," said Mrs. Coxwell. "Hello, Dorothy, Ruth. We're so sorry for your loss."

"Thank you," said Mom. "Hi, Mary. Thanks for coming."

"Of course," Mary said, as she hugged my mom.

There was a constant stream of people in and out of Mom's living room. The Wilsons came followed by the Greens. Aunt Geraldine tried to talk to the girls about wonderful memories of their mother, Janet.

"Stop that, Geraldine," said Grandpa Duncan. "We'll not have any talk of memories or death." He stood coldly by the front door.

Late on the second day of visitation, in came Dolores Bryce from the church choir, dressed in a frilly red flowered frock with matching lipstick. Mom noticed her long red nails, as she removed her black gloves. "Oh, George, I've been thinking of you. Such a tragedy. Such a loss. Call me if you need a shoulder to cry on." She never even acknowledged the girls.

At the end of the school year, Grandpa Duncan sent my mom and her sister to a relative's farm for the summer. When they returned in late August, he'd remarried.

Every trace of Mom's mother was gone. Her precious good china had been replaced, her linens were gone, and every photo that included her had disappeared. With her mother erased, Mom's home was no longer her home.

"Dorothy, Ruth, this is my wife, Dolores Bryce - now Dolores Duncan," my grandfather announced. "But I want you to call her 'Mom'," my grandfather announced to his daughters.

"Hello, girls. Why don't you give me a kiss?" said Dolores. The girls recognized her from their mother's wake. They refused to kiss her or to call her "Mom." She was always "Dolores" to them.

Things only got worse as Dolores settled in. "Dorothy," she whined. "Tidy up your room - *now*. I'm not your slave, you know."

My mom did her best to ignore her.

"Ruth, make sure you're home by ten," said Dolores in her shrill voice. "I won't tolerate lateness."

"Dad, can I be home by eleven?" asked Ruth. "Ten is too early."

"Listen to your mother, Ruth," said Grandpa.

Dolores never had children of her own and didn't seem at all interested in mothering. She would send the girls away as often as possible. My mom didn't mind being apart from Dolores, but, in losing her mother, she had lost her father, too. And being away meant being away from all her friends.

"It was such a lonely time," Mom told me years later. "And the worst of it was that harpy had had her eye on my father since my mother became ill. As soon as Mom died, she moved in for the kill."

* * *

Dolores continued to torment my mother. One Christmas, when I was twelve years old, she gave my brother half a pack of Bic pens for Christmas, saving the other half as a gift for our cousin, Jim. This was despite the fact that Grandpa Duncan had lots of money.

My brother hid his disappointment. "Wow, thank you, Grandma. Thanks, Grandpa. These will sure come in handy."

That same Christmas, Mom gave Dolores a beautiful plant. On the way out the door, Dolores threw it in the garbage in our garage.

Mom walked out to the garage later that night to put the garbage in the trash.

"Why, that ungrateful cow," she said. "Charlie, look what she did with my plant."

My mother had never even told us she wasn't our real grandmother.

Late that night, after everyone had gone home, I overheard my parents talking.

"Dot, why don't you just tell the kids that Dolores is not your real mother," my father whispered to my mom. I stood in the front hallway in my pyjamas struggling to hear. "They have a right to know, and it's just too hard for you to have to constantly avoid calling her Dolores. They need to know your mother died."

"I don't want them to call her Dolores. I don't want them to know," my mom said.

"They can still call her Grandma," Dad said. "That's what they're used to anyways."

The next day, I confronted my parents and the truth came out. Still, Mom never talked about her biological mother until years later. One day, when my mom was about eighty-two, she invited my two daughters and me for lunch at the Toronto Ladies Golf Club in Thornhill where she was on the board of directors. At one point, the board had urged Mom to become chair, but my mom said it was too hard working with just women because they took too long to make decisions.

"My mother was a member of this club, too, you know," Mom said. "That's why I wanted to join. When she was well, she used to take the train from Forest Hill all the way out here to play golf. She would always leave our lunch ready for us."

While it was obviously difficult for Mom to talk about her mother, she seemed relieved to open up a bit. The girls and I talked on the drive home about how privileged we felt to have heard those stories.

"I've never heard Granny talk like that about her real mother," said my daughter, Leah, then a student at university.

"I think Granny really wanted us to hear those stories," said Eliana. "I think that's why she invited us to the club today."

"Wasn't it wonderful?" I drove along thinking about how much Mom must have loved her mother.

One day, not long after that, I noticed a new framed photograph in my mother's living room. It was a picture of my mom at age five sitting on her mother's lap. Mom said it was the only picture she had of her mother. It had taken the death of her father and Dolores for her to get hold of it.

Unfortunately, even after Dolores was gone, she continued to haunt my mother. My grandfather had written a will leaving an inheritance to my mother and her sister. Of greatest importance, he left my real grandmother's good china to my mother. After his death, however, Dolores somehow managed to have a new will written that left all Grandpa Duncan's money to her side of the family, along with my grandmother's dishes. Mom was furious and heartbroken.

"How can that woman continue to plague me even after her death?" she wailed. It mattered so much to my mother that she hired a lawyer to fight for those dishes. It wasn't the cottage she wanted. It wasn't the money. It was a piece of her beloved mother that she yearned for. The case went on for months. Finally, after spending thousands and thousands of dollars on legal fees, my mother won back those treasured dishes.

One day, not long after the legal matters were settled, my mother arrived on my doorstep with several boxes. "These are your grandmother's dishes," she said. "I know it hasn't always been easy between you and me, but I want you to have them."

"Thanks, Mom," I said. "I'm honoured. Please, let me put on some coffee." In my mom's typical fashion, she refused to stay and was off to another event. I was disappointed, but I wasn't surprised. Talking about personal things was so hard for her.

Still, it meant a lot that she gave me those dishes. To this day, they sit in a special glassed-in cabinet in our kitchen: a pair of exquisite blue and green birds sitting on branches for all to see.

8

My Father, the Music Man

Thanks to my father, music was a huge part of my childhood. We often sat around the kitchen table after dinner while he played his baritone ukulele, and the whole family sang along. Man, could my dad play. He made it look so easy with his syncopated rhythms and elaborate chords. My mother, brother, sister, and I sang with him: "Yellow Bird," "Careless Love." Sandy might sing the melody while I came in a major third above her. Duncan would add the major fifth and Mom would chime in with a major seventh. It wasn't planned. We'd never taken singing lessons; we had learned by osmosis. Those moments made me feel so loved. My father's music made me feel I could do anything.

When my parents had people over, I would lie in bed and drift off to sleep to the sound of live music coming from downstairs: beanpole Artie Mackenzie on the washtub bass, elegant Carl Williams on the piano, and Dad on his ukulele – taa, ta, ta, ta, ta, taa, taa, taa – hands clapping, fingers snapping, and toes tapping. Sometimes it felt like a minor earthquake was going on below.

One night, still awake, my sister and brother and I shuffled downstairs in our pyjamas to sing along to a song or two. Martinis were flowing and cigarette smoke danced around the room. The three of us sat in a line on one stair - all in our flannelette jammies.

"Sing us a song," Mom said taking a long draw on her Rothman's cigarette.

"Yes, kids. Charlie can play along," said Helen Lane, as she sipped her Manhattan and twirled her bobbed brown hair with her other hand."

"Let's sing 'When the Red, Red Robin comes Bob, Bo, Bobbin' Along'," said Dad. This was a song our family loved, taught to us by my father's parents. "One, two, a one, two, three ..."

"*When the red, red robin comes bob-bob bobbin, along, along,*" the three of us sang enthusiastically.

"*When the red, red robin comes bob, bob, bobbin' along, along.... Wake up, wake up you sleepy head. Get up, get up, get out of bed. Cheer up, cheer up, the sun is red. Live, love, laugh, and be happy.*"

Balding John Beatty sprawled on the couch, sipped his beer and smiled.

"Oh kids, that's fantastic," said lofty Shirley Mackenzie, as she put out her cigarette and reached for her rye and ginger.

"Sing us another one." Donald Scott, tall and handsome, stood behind the bar pouring drinks. We sang "Lemon Tree" and everyone joined in on the chorus.

"Okay, kids. Back to bed," said Mom.

"Oh, Mom. Just one more," I begged.

"Don't 'Oh, Mom' me. You know the rules."

Then the three of us climbed the stairs to bed as Dad sang "*Come to Kilcoo, when you're feeling blue. Come to Kilcoo. We'll see you through.*" He loved jazz, but his favourite was "The Kilcoo Blues" from his summer camp days.

Each year, when summer came, we headed north to Nottawasaga beach on Georgian Bay. My dad's parents had a beautiful 1920s cottage there with a screened-in dining porch. Dad would always stay for a few weeks before heading back to work in Toronto.

I would look forward to his return on weekends for his after-dinner singsongs.

One summer night, he led us in a medley of moon songs. As my relatives harmonized, the moon shone its silvery light down on us, as though it was joining in.

"*So, shine on, shine on harvest moon, up in the sky. I ain't had no lovin' since January, February, June or July.*" My grandmother's sweet soprano voice carried the harmony, as she tapped her hands in rhythmic patterns across the table. We sang and swayed, with our arms around the shoulders of our table mates.

The singing served as an invitation for relatives from neighbouring cottages to join us. Down the path they came, and we could hear their voices from outside: "*Snow time ain't no time to stay outdoors and spoon. So, shine, shine on harvest moon, for me and my gal.*"

As cousins, aunts and uncles arrived in the dining porch, we scooched over to make room on the benches. Those who couldn't fit, grabbed chairs from other rooms and joined us. Dad led us all in the singing: Verses and verses from "Paper Moon," and "Oh, Mister Moon."

It was as though the moon smiled down and finished the medley with a grand "Yeah!"

Another evening at sunset, all the cottagers gathered firewood and set an enormous bonfire -or so it seemed to me then. The children and adults grabbed lawn chairs, blankets, and marshmallows and formed a circle around the fire. The flames leapt into the sky as the fuchsia sun set beyond the horizon. With my dad at the helm, we sang for hours. Dad played his ukulele and led us in rounds of "Fire's Burning," and "In the Jungle." As the evening wind wafted through my hair, we sang "*Wimowey, A Wimowey, A Wimowey, A Wimowey*" in four-four time, while the waves reached the shore and fell back to the beat. We kids fell asleep on blankets on the sand while the adults serenaded us.

As I got a bit older, I wanted to be able to create music and instill joy like my father. When I was eleven years old, he started to teach me how to play the ukulele. I was a quick study because I had been watching and listening to him all those years.

"So, Jackie, this is a D-major chord - you'll use it in many songs." Dad placed the fingers of my left hand on the proper strings. "That's right, honey, you've got it. Good for you."

"How do I do an A chord again?" I asked.

"These three fingers here. Good. Now practise moving from D to A. Back and forth. You're great, dear. Now let's add the E chord and we'll try a new song." He gently showed me the chord and then we practised moving through all three.

"I like the way your strumming is so loose. You're a natural."

"Can we try 'If I had a Hammer?'" I asked.

"Sure, but we'll need to add a B-minor. Let me show you." He carefully placed my fingers on the strings, and then we strummed together, me following his lead. "I think you're ready." He counted me in, and we sang together, harmonizing naturally.

We played for a while longer using our new chords and some old ones and then we both put our instruments away carefully. I hugged my dad and he bent down and gave me a kiss on the cheek. He taught me with such love - Dad on his baritone uke and me on his regular ukulele. I cherished those sessions when we played and sang together - harmonizing whenever we could.

After a couple of years, I moved on to play the guitar. As I improved, Dad and I began accompanying our family singsongs together. In my later teenage years, I started singing and playing in clubs and on campuses across Ontario. I became a real folkie for a while, playing Joni Mitchell's "Big Yellow Taxi," and others, including some of my own songs. My parents were so proud of me and would regularly come to listen to me along with their friends when I played in Toronto.

One night, when I was playing at a restaurant near home called "The Copper Kettle," Mom and Dad came to hear me, along with their friends the Beattys, the Mackenzies, and the Montgomerys. My parents ordered martinis and the rest drank beer, rum and cokes, or gin and tonics.

"Yay, Jackie," my dad called out. "Play some of your own songs."

"Play the one about going out west," said my mom.

I could tell Mom and Dad had drank a few martinis before they left home. I sat on a stool wearing a floor-length flowered dress like a real hippie. I spoke into the microphone and honoured my mother's request. "This is one I wrote. It's called 'Going Nowhere Blues.'"

"Think I'll go out west and stay awhile. Kick around Vancouver style.
Maybe tomorrow, I'm gonna fly. Give me one chance and I won't stop 'til I die.
These are my 'goin' nowhere days.'"

I wasn't even halfway through when some drunk stranger yelled out, "Play 'Snowbird!'"

"Let her play what she wants," shouted my dad.

"I want to hear 'Snowbird,'" barked the stranger.

"I don't do 'Snowbird,'" I said to the man.

"Did you hear her?" said Dad. "She doesn't do 'Snowbird,' so zip it." Dad turned his attention back to me. "Go, Jackie. You play whatever you want."

I took a deep breath to calm myself and played, "Needle and the Damage Done" by Neil Young.

"Jackie, that was great," Mom slurred. "Now play something we can sing along to."

They were getting as bad as the stranger my dad had shouted down.

"Play something by Nat King Cole," said Dad.

"I don't know anything by Nat King Cole," I said in exasperation. "I'll play 'Working in a Coal Mine.' You can sing along to that."

The song started out slow and got faster and faster. As it sped up, Mom got up, came up to the stage, and started dancing and stomping her foot. I tried not to look at her and kept playing.

The manager came up to my mother. "There's no dance floor here. Please have a seat." Mom reluctantly sat down.

"Was she bothering you?" the manager asked.

"No," I said, staring at my microphone. "She's my mother."

Mom and Dad and their friends stayed for a few more hours. My parents carried on in the same way until they left. Seeing them to the door, I stood watching them weave their way down the street. Finally, I had some peace.

Decades later, Dad developed dementia. He became increasingly ill with skin cancer and other ailments and was eventually hospitalized. It was devastating seeing him like that. He would often scream out in pain, and the nurses would do what they could to soothe him. He eventually stopped eating. He didn't need his dentures anymore.

One day, my sister and I, along with our daughters, brought my guitar to Dad's hospital room and gathered around him. His once hefty build had become bony and brittle. His eyes and cheeks had sunk severely. As I played my guitar, the girls held my father's frail, almost transparent hands. Dad managed to tap his fragile fingers against the palm of my daughter's hand to keep the beat. Together, we sang some of his favourite songs including "The Kilcoo Blues," - all sung with harmony, all sung with love.

"Come to Kilcoo, when you're feeling blue.
Come to Kilcoo. We'll see you through.
Your troubles may ail you, but Kilcoo never will fail you.
Come and sing the Kilcoo Blues."

Even though he couldn't remember what he'd had for dinner, he could still remember all the words to his favourite song, "The Kilcoo Blues." When we finished, he mustered a thumbs up and spoke a few laboured, breathless words: "I'm so happy."

He died two days later, late at night, alone in his hospital room. I hoped that he still had the happiness of "The Kilcoo Blues" deep in his heart, lifting him into heaven. I can feel my dad's music to this day - the strumming of his ukulele, the warmth of his baritone voice, and the love that he gave me through song. Whenever I listen, he is still there.

The Canes in Barbados

Dad's great-great-great-grandfather sailed for sunnier climes in Barbados after graduating from Cambridge. The Honourable Joseph Batch Cane was the first in the family to emigrate from England to Barbados, where he eventually became Clerk of the Legislative Council. He and his wife had three sons, all born on the island, all three of whom studied at Cambridge, like their father.

Charles, the eldest, was Dad's great-great-grandfather. The Very Reverend Charles Cane served with the Anglican Church in Barbados, then part of the Church of England. He became Rector of St. Michael's Cathedral in Barbados in 1842 and was later elected Dean of Barbados, presiding over all eleven Anglican churches. He served at St. Michael's for fifty years and died in 1901.

Charles's brother was Sir Joseph Batch Cane, who studied law at Cambridge. He was appointed Solicitor-General of Barbados and later installed as Chief Justice of the colony. Sir Joseph Cane was knighted in 1840 by Queen Victoria for his work in helping to emancipate the slaves in Barbados. All three brothers were likely slave owners, however, and probably received reparations from the British crown after the abolition of slavery in Britain and in the colony. This is not a pleasant part of our family history, but it was a reality for whites with property in Barbados at that time.

William Cane, the third brother, became a surgeon and served with one of the British regiments in Barbados.

The citizens of Barbados must not have always looked fondly upon the three Cane brothers because Barbadian political cartoons of the time pictured them as "The Hangman," "The Grave Digger," and "The Butcher."

As a young man, my dad's grandfather, Charles Cane, and his wife, May, left Barbados and travelled from Florida to Canada by covered wagon. They were adventuresome and wanted a new life in North America. I remember my ninety-nine-year-old great-grandmother telling me stories of their journey: how she and her husband coursed bareback on horses along the beaches of Florida.

"The wind whipped through my hair as I galloped across the sand. I was just a young girl. I remember the water spraying up around my bare feet."

Great-grandpa Charles Cane settled down once they reached Toronto and took up a position at the Home Bank of Canada. When the bank went belly-up in 1923, thousands of people lost their life savings and my great-grandfather lost his job. His son, my grandfather, Joseph Edward Batch Cane, was forced to quit school and go to work.

An ambitious young man, he started his own company called Cane and Till Insurance; they mostly insured garages. This, however, was in the midst of the Great Depression, and my grandfather eventually had to give up his independence and go to work for my grandmother's father at T. Ross Jones and Company. It wasn't long before my grandfather married my grandmother, Jane Jones. They had an elegant spring wedding at Grace Church on-the-Hill in Forest Hill. Shortly after my dad was born, my grandfather moved over to Moss Lawson - a brokerage firm. He stayed with that company until his retirement at the age of 85.

Mom and Dad's Martinis

My dad loved his father and mother dearly, as we all did. Mom was particularly proud of Dad's upper-class British ancestry.

"I'll make the curried kidneys on English muffins for Christmas morning," she said to me one winter's day. "Dad's parents handed down this recipe that came from generations before them. What good taste."

I love the curried kidneys as well and still cook them every Christmas. I suppose I feel somewhat connected to my British ancestry.

10

The Gentle Giant

My dad, Charles Joseph Jones Cane, was known as "C.J.C." or "Charlie the Party Animal." He spent most of his childhood at 63 Dawlish Crescent in a grand old stone and brick home with beautiful gardens in the front and back. Dad was the eldest with a younger sister, Rose, and a baby brother, Albert.

As a young boy, he loved playing hockey with his pals. In the summers, he journeyed north to the large family cottage on Georgian Bay with its sprawling sandy beach and endless property. It was surrounded by cottages owned by aunts and friends, with wooden pathways connecting each cottage to the next.

As a teenager, Dad spent some of each summer at Camp Kilcoo on Gull Lake near Minden, Ontario. During the school year, he attended Lawrence Park Collegiate, strolling up Chatsworth Drive each day with his friends, John Beatty and Ken Montgomery. Dad was a flanker on his high school football team; tall, blond John Beatty was the team's quarterback.

"Johnny," Dad said to him at a game one afternoon, "no one's covering me because you're not throwing the ball my way. Please, throw to me. Now's our chance."

John took my dad's advice. Sure enough, Dad was wide open. He caught the ball and ran in for a touchdown.

"We did it, Johnny," Dad cheered, as he gave John a congratulatory slap on the back.

"You're right, Charlie. Great going," said John.

It was one of Dad's favourite stories at the dinner table, often accompanied by, "I've got dentures because of my football career."

John Beatty later told us that Dad never lost a single tooth playing football - he just had bad teeth. I was a bit shocked that Dad had lied to us, but I guess, my father had visions of a much greater football experience.

Then it was off to the University of Toronto for my Dad. There, he met his lifelong friends, Artie Mackenzie, Jim Baldwin, and Donald Scott. They were the ones who dubbed him "The Shadow" when he met Mom.

After my father graduated from U of T, he took an industrial sales job in Montreal. Dad drove his old Chevrolet all over town making cold call after cold call. Finally, he made his first huge sale, selling tens of thousands of nuts and bolts. He was so excited at his success that he forgot his parked car and ran all the way back to his office to tell his boss.

Excitement aside, it wasn't long before Dad realized that industrial sales wasn't for him. He wanted to deal with people on a regular basis and he had a great head for numbers. Soon, Canada Life came calling. My dad sold life insurance with them for fifty-five years. As a dedicated salesman who always strove to be the best, it didn't take him long to become a member of an elite club known as the Million Dollar Round Table. Members of this venerable group each sold one million dollars in insurance annually. Once Dad achieved his membership in the MDRT, he never wanted to miss a year, and he never did. In fact, he consistently sold the most policies each year for all of Canada Life.

Dad was asked to speak at numerous Canada Life conventions and to share his successes and strategies. Of course, these conventions weren't all work. The people attending them became an integral part of Mom and Dad's social circle. Dad brought his ukulele and led singsongs in his hotel room after the sessions were done for the day. Through all the fun, however, conscientiousness and integrity were the traits that defined my father the most.

My father also enjoyed his colleagues back at the office. Every Friday at lunch, Dad and Mario Romano and the gang gathered at Tony's Italian Restaurant at Queen and Simcoe. Tony's was a classic, with its red and white checkered tablecloths and dark-wood interior - they always took the same corner booth. "Can we get another round of your bathtub martinis?" Dad asked the waiter one Friday afternoon.

"Yeah, this round's on me," Mario Romano said, as he stroked his black hair back and loosened his tie. "I've got something to tell you."

"I hope you're not leaving Canada Life," said Dad.

"No, it's worse than that," said Mario.

"What is it?" asked tall, lean Bill Gordon.

Jimmy looked around at the group. "I've got lung cancer. It's not good," said Mario.

"Jesus, Mario. How long have you known?" asked Dad.

"I just found out. I haven't even told Anna, and I don't know if I will."

"Can they treat it?" asked Bill.

"No, there's nothing they can do. I've just got to enjoy whatever time I've got left. They've given me a few months."

"Mario - I don't know what to say," said Dad. "Maybe you should get a second opinion." He gulped back his martini. "Waiter, we'll get another round. This one's definitely on me."

"I did get a second opinion."

The group sat in awkward silence for a moment. Then, the next round arrived.

"In buona salute," said Mario in his typical dark humour. "To good health."

Mario Romano died two months later. I went to the funeral with my parents. Dad felt sick about losing one of his best pals. I kept glancing over at him during the service, looking for the tears, but somehow, they never came.

* * *

In addition to breaking records at his job, Dad found time to be a sports fanatic. He and my mother curled, skied, golfed, and played tennis together and separately. When Dad was home, the television set was always on, set to some game. My siblings and I used to joke that he invented the television converter. Dad loved to lie on his bed Saturday and Sunday afternoons, have a nap, and watch television. One of us was usually watching TV in the room below Mom and Dad's bedroom. Dad had developed a code. If he banged his foot on the floor several times, it meant that he wanted the channel changed. Whichever one of us heard the banging was expected to run upstairs to my dad's bedroom and change the channel as directed.

Eventually we had four televisions so that my father could move from room to room without missing a play. It left little opportunity for meaningful conversation. It also made me feel invisible.

One Sunday night, when we were eating on TV tables in front of the television, I accidentally walked in front of the TV.

"Jesus Christ, Jackie," Dad yelled. "Get out of the way. I can't see the set." I lost my appetite. It turned me off television for years.

One Saturday night, Dad was watching the hockey game during a terrible storm. Lightning struck the television set and blew up the tube. With sparks flying in all directions, my dad jumped up, ran out the family room door into the backyard and yelled, "Dot, get the kids!"

Mom followed Dad out into the backyard. "Charlie, come back in the house."

"Are the kids okay?" he asked, as he made his way back into the family room.

"Everyone's fine. The TV's fried though."

"Oh, my God, my television."

"At least there wasn't a fire."

"We'll have to get a new set on Monday," said Dad. "I'm going up to watch the rest of the game upstairs. I hope that set is okay."

It wasn't the only sport-related mishap in our home. Another time, my dad was playing catch with my brother on the lawn at the side of our house. Dad threw the ball and it smashed right through the neighbour's basement window. My father grabbed my brother. "Let's get out of here." He and my brother ran in through our back door to hide.

"What are we going to do, Dad?" asked my brother, as my father paced back and forth in front of the piano.

"I'll have to go next door and tell Mr. White," he said. "It's the right thing to do. Wish me luck."

Off Dad walked, across the lawn to where Mr. White was picking up pieces of glass.

"Hey, Jack. Sorry about that. David and I had a bit of an accident playing catch. Actually, I threw the ball. Let me help you clean up this mess. I'll obviously pay for the window."

Even though it took my dad some time before he confessed to the neighbor about the window, it was just like him to do the right thing.

Dad was generally a happy man who loved his family and friends. Even though he had many evening appointments for work, he always came home for a family dinner before going back to work.

Mom always had a beautiful meal on the table every night and the entire family would sit down together to eat.

"Dinner, kids," she called one weeknight. Dad came and sat at the head of the table. Mom put the plates in front of my father and sat down at the other end.

"Yummy, meatloaf," Duncan said, as he sat down on his side of the table. "My favourite." Sandy and I took our seats on the other side.

"Okay, kids, guess where I had lunch today?" said Dad, as he served the meatloaf and passed the plate down to my mother who was serving the mashed potatoes and salad.

"Hy's Steak House?" Duncan knew the drill - guessing where Dad had lunched and what he had eaten was a nightly ritual.

"Nope," said Dad.

"I know, Tony's for Italian," I said.

"Nope. Not Tony's," my father said. "We only go there on Friday's."

"I know," said Sandy. "You went to Ed's Warehouse."

"You're right. Now, what did I eat?"

"I bet you ate roast-beef," said Duncan.

"You've got it," said Dad. "What came with the roast-beef?"

"Oh, this is too hard," I complained.

"We've all been to Ed's Warehouse for the roast-beef," said Mom. "You should be able to remember."

"We're having one of the things tonight," said Dad.

"Mashed potatoes," said Duncan.

"Right," said Dad. "What else?"

"Green beans," I said.

"Peas," said Sandy. "And gravy."

"Right on both counts. Now, there's one more thing. It's very British."

"It starts with a 'Y'," said Mom.

There was silence for a moment.

"Oh, I know," Duncan yelled. "Yorkshire pudding."

"You've got it," said Dad. "Good for you."

When Duncan was young, my dad coached his hockey team. My mom, my sister, and I attended every game, spending endless hours in cold arenas sipping coffee or hot chocolate.

"You can't make a call like that," I remember Dad hollering. "What kind of a ref are you?" My dad set the record for bench penalties for yelling at the referee. My poor brother's teammates were constantly being put in the penalty box for my father's misdemeanors.

Years passed, and Dad had seven grandchildren, including two grandsons, Robbie and Victor. He went on to attend all of their hockey games, too. Dad sometimes even travelled to Connecticut to watch Robbie play on his university team.

As Dad aged, his knees bothered him more and more. He had knee surgery, but was never the same after that. He didn't do the exercises required to get his knee functioning again and eventually required a walker. Then, dementia set in.

"Dot ... Dot! Where are you, Dot?" Dad yelled for my mother one afternoon. He was lying on his bed trying to nap as he usually did.

"Charlie, stop yelling at me," said Mom, as she came into the bedroom. "What do you want?"

"Where were you?" he asked.

"I'm just making phone calls. I'm not going anywhere." Back she went to the den.

"Dot?" my father called out again. "Dot! Come here, Dot!"

"I'm on the phone," yelled Mom. "Please stop yelling at me."

"Dot, I need you!"

My mother ignored him, but he kept yelling out.

When they finally hired a caregiver it became, "Bailey ... Bailey!" Years later, when my mom gave up the will to live, I'm sure it had to do with the deterioration of life at home. Once Mom died, all Dad did was sleep and eat and get up for his five o'clock martinis.

My husband Ivan and I and our children began taking my dad to the local Swiss Chalet for Sunday night dinners. "When are we going to that chicken place?" Dad would often ask. The only problem was that Swiss Chalets didn't make gin martinis. They didn't carry vermouth. There was only one way to deal with that dilemma. I started bringing a water bottle of vermouth in a tote bag.

"I'll have a double shot of gin on ice," Dad said to the server one night. "Okay, Jackie, work your magic."

I took Dad's glass and held it under the table. My daughter Eliana opened the vermouth and poured a dab into Dad's glass. Back on top of the table, we added a teaspoon of water and voila -Dad had a perfect martini. My father loved the game, and I didn't feel guilty because he was drinking a lot less when he was out with us than he did at home alone. We kept those weekly trips to Swiss Chalet going until he was no longer healthy enough to go out.

He became increasingly cantankerous as his dementia progressed.

When he ended up in hospital for skin cancer and other complications, Dad developed a reputation for his terrible temper and lack of patience.

He constantly rang the nurse's call button.

"Nurse ... I need a nurse. I need a nurse now!"

"Yes, Mr. Cane. What is it you need now? I was just here."

"I'm thirsty. I need something to drink."

"I'll get you something in a minute. I've got lots of other patients, you know."

While one nurse was attempting to feed my dad, he kicked her in the stomach. The doctor eventually gave him some anti-anxiety medication - something I thought he had needed long before then - and he calmed down significantly.

One day, while Ivan and I and our three children were visiting him, he seemed relatively cheerful. Even though he was extremely sick and frail, when we rose to go, he called out to Ivan, "Good to see you, my man." And, turning his attention to the kids, "Bye Eliana, Leah, Victor. So good of you to come today." As we left and walked down the hall, we heard my father sing out to the nurses in his bold baritone, "I need a drink of water." It was as though he was singing a solo in a choir. Who could resist that? We went back and got him a drink.

11

The Water Spider

In adulthood, as in her childhood, Mom was a mover and a shaker. When we were really young, Mom was chair of the Home and School Committee at our elementary school. Once we were teenagers, Mom took on a huge volunteer role with the Art Gallery of Ontario. She and her friend, Doris Caldicott, orchestrated the first lottery in Ontario. It was 1970, and the AGO wanted to build an extension. Mom was co-chair of the committee with the task of making it happen. We had to have a separate phone line added at home, so Mom could access her calls. She was constantly organizing media events to publicize the AGO lottery. It was a huge gamble. Only the Irish Sweepstakes existed back then, and many people didn't think lotteries should be legal.

One afternoon, Mom was driving the artist Harold Town to speak on CFRB's Betty Kennedy show - a well-known radio talk show. Harold Town was a highly acclaimed abstract painter and printmaker whose works showed in the AGO and art galleries around the world. He was a deeply sensitive and eccentric man.

Mom was driving the beat-up old red Mercedes Benz she and my dad had bought in a used car lot. The car rarely got from A to

B. In true Dot Cane fashion, she picked Harold up late and they had to boot it to the studio.

"Don't mind me," he said to my mother. He leaned his tall, skinny frame back to sit rigidly in his seat, then gripped the overhead handle with one hand, and nervously stroked his thick beard with the other.

As Mom, stepped on the gas, Harold's entire seat thrust backwards into the back seat. When she put her foot on the brake, he propelled forward, hitting his head on the dashboard. Seat belts were almost unheard of in those days.

"Sorry," said Mom. "Hold on." As Mom gave the car some gas, Harold flew backwards. She hit the brakes. Forwards. Backwards. Forwards. All the way to the studio.

"Shit," he yelled. "You drive like a mad woman. Let me out. I'll walk."

"No time for that." Mom hit the gas. "The show airs in ten minutes. We're almost there."

Mom parked the car and led Harold into the CFRB radio studio.

"You're late," Betty Kennedy said to Harold. "We need to get you seated and do a sound check with your microphone."

"I'm just telling you now," said Harold. "I'm not driving back with her. I'll take the subway. The bus, anything - I'll walk."

In spite of her driving reputation, Mom made sure the AGO met its goals - millions of dollars of lottery tickets were sold, and the AGO built its addition at the corner of Dundas and McCaul streets. After this success, the states of New York and California hired Mom to set up lotteries there. Mom then continued on with paid work as fundraiser for the University of Toronto's sesquicentennial campaign. From there, she was hired to raise funds for the Young People's Theatre in Toronto.

When she wasn't working, she played her sports and, in later years, played bridge. She also had a regular group of about ten women who gathered once a month at each other's homes for a night of poker. The cigarette smoke would swirl in the air and the ladies' drinking could match that of any of their male counterparts. Each woman would come with a bag of hundreds of pennies in a purple felt and gold Crown Royal rye bag.

"How are your girls doing, Joan?" Shirley Mackenzie asked one night at our house, as she threw some pennies into the pot.

"All good," said Joan Beatty, as she took a long drag on her cigarette and stood up to pour herself another gin and tonic.

Mary Baldwin sipped her scotch. "Dot, did you say Jackie was in a play?"

"Yes, she's got a lead in her high school musical," said Mom. "She's walking around the house singing her solos constantly." She took a good swig of her martini. "I used to direct, produce, and even star in the UC Follies at U of T. Those were good times." Mom had a way of bringing the conversation around to herself.

At about eleven o'clock, Mom brought out finger sandwiches and served coffee. After that, the women considered themselves sober enough to get in their cars and drive home. This was a monthly ritual that went on for fifty years.

12

The Dark Times I

When John F. Kennedy was assassinated, my grade three teacher told us at the end of the school day. I wandered home filled with so many questions. When I got home, I immediately told my mother that the President of the United States had been killed.

"Yes, I know," she said without looking at me. She continued to stir the pot on the stove.

"Why did someone kill him, Mom?" I asked.

"I don't know, Jackie." She took the spoon and tasted the spaghetti sauce. "I don't want to talk about it."

"What will happen to his children?"

"I said, 'I don't want to talk about it.'" Mom added some salt to the sauce. "Get yourself a snack and go practise piano. Go on. And don't mention it again."

I had no appetite for a snack and went down to the piano. I played a child's version of Beethoven's "Moonlight Sonata" to soothe my aching soul. Over and over again, I played it. Then I went to my room and just lay on my bed, staring at the wall. Later, we sat at dinner and talked about where Dad had eaten lunch like we usually did. There was no mention of John F. Kennedy.

Days went by and a copy of *Time* magazine with a picture of Kennedy on the cover came to the house. I found it on the kitchen table and took it downstairs to the family room and sat there alone. I looked closely at the pictures of Kennedy's funeral. There was his wife, Jackie, dressed all in black with a sheer black veil over her face. Beside her, daughter Carolyn wore a light-blue dress coat and little red shoes. Finally, there was tiny son John dressed in a similar blue coat and short pants saluting his father's casket. Why did this happen, I wondered. Why would God do this to a family? I looked at the pictures over and over again. I could hear a TV on somewhere in the house, and, at one point, my mother's heels clicked across the floor. No one came down to join me, though.

* * *

When I was ten years old, I discovered I loved to draw. For some reason, one night I drew a picture of Montreal's mayor, Jean Drapeau. It was the spitting image of him with his jowls, mustache, bald head, and black-rimmed square glasses. I have no idea why I drew that kind of a picture when I was so young. All I know is that I worked very hard on it, and I was proud. I took it down to the dining room where Mom and Dad were sitting, sipping after-dinner martinis. I showed Dad the picture.

"Who's this supposed to be?" Dad asked, his breath reeking of gin.

"It's the mayor of Montreal," I said. "I guess I should have drawn it better."

"Don't you like it?" He wobbled in his chair. He had a horrible frown on his face.

"Well, I guess I could have done a better job."

With that, Dad took the picture and slowly ripped it right down the middle.

I was stunned.

Mom and Dad's Martinis

"There. I hope you've learned your lesson," Dad said, handing me back the torn portrait. "If you like something, say you like it. If you're proud, say you're proud. Now go to your room."

I looked to my mother, but she said nothing and kept on drinking her martini.

Heartbroken, I took the destroyed picture up to my room and tried to tape the two halves back together. It wasn't the same. I spent days trying to recreate that drawing, but I couldn't do it. Eventually, I hid the taped picture in the back of my drawing book and drew a picture of a snowman instead. My dad never said another word about it, and neither did I.

* * *

I got in a lot of trouble as a teenager. When I was sixteen, I joined the high school cheerleading squad. After a winning game, I convinced most of the squad members to join me at the Algonquin Tavern near our school. Six of us crowded into a booth in our orange turtle necks and brown jumpers, with orange pompoms on our white running shoes. Flashing the driver's licence of a friend's older sister, I ordered a couple of pitchers of beer. After we'd had a few drinks, we started jumping up and down doing our cheerleading kicks and calling out, "We've got the T.E.A.M. that's on the B.E.A.M. We've got the team that's on the beam that's really hip to the jive, so come on Jackson - skin 'em alive."

Two older men came over to join us. "What's your name?" one of them asked me.

"Jacelyn. I mean, Sheila."

"Well, which is it?"

"Sheila. It's Sheila."

"How old are you, Sheila?" He stroked his mustache with his forefinger and stuck his other hand in the pocket of his jacket.

"I'm twenty-one." That was the drinking age back then.

"Yeah, what year where you born?"

"1952, no 1950," I said.

"That makes you twenty. Let's see some I.D." He and his partner pulled out their badges.

I pulled out my fake I.D.

"When's your birthday, Sheila?" he asked.

"Um, August - no September 20, 1949." I squirmed in my seat.

"Wrong again. According to this, you were born on December 5, 1948."

"Okay, girls," said the other officer, standing up, as he pushed his hand through his blond hair. "Everyone, get your I.D. out." The other girls pulled out their own identification. "You're all under arrest for drinking under age. Let's go. We're taking you down to the station."

We were all processed and charged. They never called our parents, but told us we would each be receiving trial notices in the mail. Then the two officers drove us home - three in one cop car and three in another. As I sat in my uniform, in the back of the car, all I could do was cry.

About a month later, the notice outlining my court date and the charges against me came in the mail. I was able to intercept it without either of my parents noticing. That afternoon after school, however, I lay down on my bed and fell asleep. I had been reading the notice from the police before I slept, and for some stupid reason, I left it lying on my bedside table.

Mom came in later to wake me up for dinner. When I awoke, she was standing beside me reading the letter. "Charlie," she called. "We've got trouble. Come into the kitchen, young lady."

Mom and Dad and I sat at the kitchen table. She was furious. He was calm.

"Well, you're on your own, Jacelyn," my mom said. "I'm not going to help you get out of this one."

"I'll go with you to court," said Dad. "What were you thinking, Jackie? Going to a bar in your cheerleading outfit?"

"I didn't think I would get caught," I said.

"That's right," he said. "You didn't think."

When the trial date came, Dad and I went to the courthouse and sat together on the hard wooden seats. The entire courtroom was decorated in dark wood, including the judge's raised bench and chair. When he entered, we all stood. An older man with a curly thatch of grey hair and a voluminous black robe told me to stand, as he read out the charges. "Is there anyone here to speak on behalf of Jacelyn Cane?" he asked.

Dad stood up beside me. We were both dressed very formally. "I'm Jacelyn Cane's father, and I'm here to speak on her behalf," he said. "She is a good daughter and a very nice person. She does well at school and is very involved there."

I felt so grateful that my father spoke so kindly about me.

"That's all well and good," said the judge, "but that doesn't speak to why she chose to consume alcohol at the Algonquin Tavern five years under age." The judge continued, "I think it's clear that a fine against Jacelyn Cane would merely be a fine against her father. I therefore declare that Jacelyn Cane will be on probation for one year, beginning now. The clerk will give her the name of her probation officer whom she will visit every month. No alcohol is to be consumed during that time. Case dismissed."

Dad and I drove home. "Thanks for coming, Dad," I said.

Dad didn't look at me. "Just make sure to go to that probation officer every month."

Mom never asked me how the trial went or what punishment I had received. I assume she found out from my father. After that day, my father never spoke of the incident again. Neither of them ever asked if I was visiting my probation officer, which I did faithfully for the next year.

* * *

When I was eighteen years old and in grade thirteen, I went out with my boyfriend and came home at about two o'clock in the morning.

"Get in here," yelled Dad, as I came in the house. It was one of their rare weekend nights home, and they were in bed.

I walked down the hall and into their bedroom. "What?" I asked, giving them a bit of attitude.

Mom lay on her side with her eyes closed while Dad was propped up on his pillows, glaring. "Who do you think you are, coming in here ninety minutes after curfew? We've been sick with worry."

"I'm sorry. I didn't think you'd be awake," I said. "The time got away from me."

"Don't give me that crap." He sat up at the side of the bed. I could smell the gin. "You knew we'd be upset. Well, you're grounded. Now get out of here."

As I walked down the hall, he yelled after me, "You love to stir the pot, don't you?"

"Shut up," I shouted, as I reached my bedroom.

Dad came running after me in his pyjamas. "You little bitch! You don't talk to me like that."

I was frightened now. I turned around and he punched me in the mouth - hard. I fell back on my bed. I put my hands up to protect myself because my father looked like he was going to hit me again. "That'll teach you to talk to me like that."

My mother appeared behind him. "Charlie, what did you do to her?" she cried. "My God." She pulled him away. "Leave her alone. Come on, come back to bed."

"She had it coming," Dad said, as Mom pulled him down the hallway to their bedroom.

Neither one of them helped me as I stumbled down the hall into the bathroom. Blood dripped everywhere. I took a towel and wet it with cold water and sat on the edge of the tub trying to stop the bleeding. I sat there for fifteen minutes or more as blood oozed from my mouth and my nose. Eventually it stopped. My mother and father were asleep or at least silent. I walked back to my bedroom. Moving carefully, I packed up a bag.

At about three-thirty in the morning, I arrived at my friend Jill's house. Her mother opened the front door. My whole face was swollen by this point. I told her what had happened, and she invited me in. Jill came downstairs and the three of us sat at the kitchen table drinking tea. Black mascara ran down my cheeks as my tears streamed over my swollen face. I jumped when the phone rang.

"Hi, Charlie," said Jill's mother. "Yes, she's here. I don't think it's a good idea for you to speak to her right now. She's going to stay here for a couple of days - just to let things cool down."

After three days, I still didn't want to go home. I went from one friend's house to another, still in shock. I didn't want anyone at school to see my face. It was the week of our final grade thirteen exams, and I missed them all.

On the eighth day, I went home in the early afternoon when I knew my father wouldn't be there. My mother came out of the kitchen. "I'm glad you're home. Are you okay?"

"I just came to get my guitar and some more things. I'll be leaving."

"Why don't you come into the kitchen and play me a few songs," she said.

"I think I'll just play in my room, thanks." I closed my bedroom door. The blood on my bedspread was gone. I sat on the edge of my bed and began writing a song:

"Little girl, little girl, living downtown.
Little girl, little girl, eyes chocolate brown.
Little girl, little girl, hair gently blows.
Little girl, little girl, nobody knows."

About half an hour later, there was a knock on my bedroom door. "What?" I said.

"Can I come in?" It was my father. My mother had called and told him I was home.

"Not if you're going to hit me."

Dad came in and sat down on my bed. "Your face looks bad. I'm sorry, Jackie." Tears started to roll down his cheeks. "I'm so very sorry." He began to rock back and forth. I had never seen my father cry before. I felt terrible - and helpless. "Your mother is so mad at me. I don't know if she'll ever forgive me. Please, Jackie. You've got to make it all right."

I've got to make it all right, I thought. He wasn't feeling badly about hurting me; he was feeling badly for himself. I felt guilty and angry at the same time.

"Don't cry, Dad," I said.

"Can you talk to your mother - make it okay again?" he begged.

"I don't have anything to say to her," I said.

"Well, at least don't leave again. Please, we can't take it."

"I'll think about it," I said. "But, I need you to leave me alone. I'm writing a song."

"Can I give you a hug?"

"Maybe another day."

"I love you, Jackie."

I hesitated for a moment. "I love you, too."

Dad left the room and I continued writing my song.

Little girl, little girl, nobody knows.

In the end, I couldn't think of anywhere else to go. Once again, there was never another word about what he had done.

* * *

I was twenty-one when I realized my parents were alcoholics. When we were young, their drinking seemed more controlled - or at least I didn't notice it as much. They were the only family I knew, so their drinking seemed normal. They always had their martinis before dinner, and dinner was often very late, but we ate together, and mealtimes were generally civil. As Duncan, Sandy, and I got older, however, my parents often ate later than we did, so the drinking continued into the night. Mom always had dinner

Mom and Dad's Martinis

prepared before she started drinking. That way, she only had the last-minute touches to worry about.

One night, Mom was banging around the kitchen, as she put dinner on the table for herself and my father. She was so drunk. By about nine o'clock, they sat down in the kitchen to eat. I heard them talking from my bedroom.

"Charles, why don't we invest in John Beatty's hovercraft business?" said Mom. "I think it's really going to be a success."

"Dot, dry up," said Dad. "I'm not investing in something so risky. You don't know what you're talking about."

"Yes, I do," said Mom. "John's got good business sense."

"Shut up, motor mouth."

"Tom, it's my money, too."

"It's not your money. It's my money." He took another sip of his martini. "I worked hard all my life for this money."

"Well, I've worked hard all my life too," Mom responded, as she cut into her pork chop. "I've supported all of your hard work. I've raised three kids. I've cooked, I've cleaned, I've ironed. I've worked as a volunteer."

"Don't give me that crap!" he yelled. "Your whole life has been one big vacation."

I felt sick to my stomach. I hated hearing my father put my mother down like that.

Not long afterwards, I decided to write them a letter.

"Dear Mom and Dad,"

"I love you both very much, but am very concerned about your drinking. I think it is out of control. You drink every night and I think you are both alcoholics. Could we please talk about how to solve this problem?

Love, Jackie"

After my parents were asleep, I left the letter on my mom's beside table, so they would read it in the morning when they were sober.

She was making breakfast when I walked into the kitchen the next morning. Sandy was away at school at the time and Duncan was still in bed. Silence.

"Mom, can we talk?"

"I have nothing to say to you," she said.

"Good morning, Jackie," Dad said, as he came in to eat his breakfast.

"Don't speak to her, Charles," said Mom.

Dad stopped talking to me, and the three of us ate breakfast in silence. That night at cocktail time, I heard Dad whisper to Mom in the kitchen, "Should I make us a martini, Dot? Maybe we shouldn't have one."

"You're damn right we're going to have one. Don't listen to her."

My heart ached.

Dad went down to the bar and made them each a martini.

My mother went several days without speaking to me. My parents continued on with their regular martinis and never said another word about my letter. Talking about problems was not something we did well in our house.

13

Over the Chair

We grew up on Mozart Avenue in the leafy suburb of Willowdale, Ontario. Christmases were wonderful. Dad always had one of us help him put red and white Christmas lights on the evergreens on the front lawn. He insisted that his helper stand there the entire time while he balanced on the ladder, meticulously arranging the bulbs.

"Jesus Christ, Jackie," he hollered down to me when the line of lights went dead. "Check every bulb. And, for Christ sakes, make sure not to break them." Together we located the culprit, and once again the lights shone splendidly. Then we moved to the back balcony and put blue and green lights on the Christmas tree Dad had placed there, so you could see it through the glass when you walked in the front door.

Meanwhile, Mom decorated the spiral staircase, inching down the stairs backwards on her knees, tying pine boughs to the railing with stiff red bows. And the bows were just the beginning. On the bar, she displayed the porcelain Christmas Santa that made music when you wound it up. It had been in the family for generations. She carefully placed the china crèche on top of the piano. I particularly loved the Christmas card stand she set up in the front hall. It was in the shape of a Christmas tree and held cards on its branches. I looked at its additions every morning and felt warmed by the love of family and friends. A week before Christmas, we put up a real Christmas tree that reached to the ceiling.

"Now, kids, remember not to ever put your finger in the socket of a light that doesn't have a bulb," Dad said, as he put the lights on the indoor tree. "You'll get a terrible shock." He reminded us every year. It only made me want to try it to see what a shock felt like.

"Okay girls, time to decorate the tree," said Mom. "Jackie, why don't you choose a Christmas album?"

I put on Ella Fitzgerald's greatest Christmas hits and "O Holy Night" played in the background.

"Remember girls, the balls are very breakable," said Mom. "Put the red and gold ones on so they look balanced."

"I love this one of Santa," I said. "He's so chubby and happy."

"Can I put the angel on top?" said Sandy. "Jackie put it on last year."

"Go ahead, Sandy," said Mom. "Get the step ladder."

"Can we put the garland on now?" I asked. "That's my favorite part." By this time Ella was singing "Joy to the World." Mom got out the silver garland, and together we placed it delicately on the tree. The three of us stood back and admired our creation.

On Christmas Eve, the whole family piled into Dad's car and headed down to Timothy Eaton for the midnight church service. The church was in darkness except for the candlelight and the lights behind the stained-glass windows. Singing "Silent Night" with my family always made me cry. We went up to the communion rail together, where the minister administered the holy sacraments of bread and wine. Kneeling there as the organ played, I felt such love for my family and for God.

On the way home, we stopped in at the Beatty's house. John and Joan Beatty were long-time friends of my parents, and, along with their five daughters, always had a Christmas Eve gathering. Their house was beautifully decorated with candles on top of the fireplace. A roaring fire burned brightly. Joan had out a wide selection of cheese and crackers for nibbling. Friends and family were seated on couches and chairs, and on the floor.

"Come and sit here, Jackie," said Sally, the eldest Beatty, and my close friend. "Dad is going to read, 'The Night Before Christmas.'"

Mr. Beatty opened the book. "Gather round, everybody. The story is about to begin." Everyone who was standing sat down, and the room went quiet. "Twas the night before Christmas, when all through the house - not a creature was stirring, not even a mouse ...."

Once John had finished the reading, we headed home for the last big sleep before Christmas morning. Even as teenagers, we weren't allowed to go downstairs until Dad had checked to see if Santa had come.

"I've got hot chocolate and coffee," Mom said, wearing a shimmering light-blue housecoat that only came out on Christmas Day. She put out some homemade shortbread cookies to eat while we opened our presents. The gifts were piled high under the tree. We were very fortunate.

"Everyone, put your presents away while I cook," Mom said, as she stood over the frying pan. She pushed the slices of veal kidneys around in the pan and added flour. Our Christmas breakfast was very British. "Okay, I'm making the sauce. Jackie, can you come and broil the English muffins?"

I put the English muffins under the broiler.

"Watch them carefully, so they don't burn," said Mom.

Within minutes, we sat down to curried veal kidneys on English muffins. On the side, we had crumpets and jam.

My mother was a fabulous hostess, and, as a result, family Christmas dinners were almost always at our house. Grandparents, aunts, uncles, and cousins arrived at our place at five o'clock and Mom had a game for us to play to get everybody chatting. She pinned a picture of a person from a magazine on everyone's back. Each picture was part of a pair. We had to walk around and ask questions about the picture on our own back until we guessed who it was and then found our partner.

"Is it a man?" I asked my Uncle Sam.

"Yes, it is."

"Does he live in Canada?" I continued.

"No, he doesn't," he said, resting his hands on his large belly.

"England?" I asked.

"Yes."

"Is it Prince Phillip?"

"No, but close."

"Prince Charles?"

"Yes, the heir to the throne."

"Now, I've got to find my partner. Maybe Princess Anne."

There were twenty people at Christmas dinner and the table stretched from the dining room into the living room. Mom set the table beautifully. She took the gold-rimmed china out of the hutch very carefully and placed the plates by the oven where she would warm them later. Using her apron, she polished each knife before she set it down. She gently handled the red-and-green tinted glasses that my dad's mother had given her, making sure they were positioned just so on the white linen cloth. After taking the beautiful flower arrangement out of the box from the florist and placing it in the middle of the table, she stood back and admired her work. There was just one more thing - homemade nametags at every person's place.

Mom cooked the entire meal herself in those days. She stood over the stove and made turkey gravy just before dinner - her martini in one hand and a spoon in the other. Once the last-minute meal preparations were done, she lit the candles and we all sat down for Mom's famous Christmas soup made of beef and tomato broth with vermouth and sugar. Each bowl was served with a garnish of lemon and parsley. This was followed by a huge turkey, mashed potatoes, turnip, peas, and bread pudding for the first course. For dessert, we had English trifle and plum pudding which my mom brought out flaming. This was followed by liqueurs and coffee.

"Dot, that was a beautiful dinner," my Dad's mother said.

"Why, thanks, Mom," said my mother. She aimed to please my dad's parents. My grandmother was a wonderful cook.

Following dinner, the entire group moved downstairs and gathered around the piano. Mom played Christmas carols and we handed out hymn books and carol sheets. Everyone sang together for about an hour.

Then the dancing began. Dad played "Daddy" by Sammy Kaye on the stereo - one of his favourite tunes.

All the women and girls in the family lined up across the parquet floor of the family room and danced a line dance. Dad, now in his shirtsleeves and a loosened tie, and fueled by quite a few martinis, did a free-style dance around the line dancers. By that time of the night, he was wearing a hat that lit up. When the instrumental part of the song came around, he mimicked the trumpet and trombone players, dancing all the while.

Later, Mom took to the dance floor with my Uncle Fred. He was a small man who had been a paratrooper and POW in World War Two. He and my mom were jiving to Bette Midler's remake of Glenn Miller's "In the Mood." Mom was much larger back then and she took the lead. She gave my Uncle Fred such a spin that he did a full somersault over an arm chair and landed on the other side. We all ran over to make sure he was all right. "I may have a bruise or two, but otherwise I'm okay," he said. "I survived Hitler, and the Nazis, but I may not survive dancing with Dot." We helped him up and laughed all night about the spectacle.

Around eleven o'clock, our own teenage friends arrived and joined the party. My best friend, Judy, arrived with her long flaming-red curls. She suggested we drink the remnants of wine in the glasses on the dining room table. We were only fifteen.

"Just make sure no one sees us." I said. Everyone else was downstairs dancing. The two of us polished off about ten partially-full glasses.

"There's more in the decanter," said Judy, as she poured some out into one of the glasses.

"Pour me some."

We finished it off and wobbled downstairs to join the party.

Gradually, the relatives made their way home, but the party continued. Dad stood on the stairs leading all of our friends in Ike and Tina Turner's "Proud Mary." He sang Tina's part as he danced. Eventually he and Mom went to bed and we stayed up partying.

On Boxing Day morning, Dad came out to the kitchen and almost wept at the sight of the turkey carcass. "Duncan!" he hollered. "Get up here!" Duncan's bedroom was on the lower level and he knew to come running when my dad called.

"What?" asked my brother.

"What's happened to my turkey? There's not even enough meat on here for sandwiches."

"Sorry, Dad," said Duncan. "My friends nibbled on it last night. I didn't realize they ate so much."

I think that may have been the last time our friends were invited to come over on Christmas night.

Then Dad ran down to the family room to check his bar fridge. He shouted, "Duncan, Joanne, Ginny – all of you, get down here!" The three of us scrambled downstairs. Dad had noticed that all the beer was gone. "Your friends drank every last beer." My father then moved over to his liquor cabinet and held up bottles of rum, vodka, and even his cherished gin. This time he really looked like he was going to cry. "And…and." Dad could hardly get the words out. "They drank all of my liquor."

Later in the day, once my father had calmed down a bit, he started referring to our friends as the "big straws."

Years passed, and Sandy and Duncan and I all married and began having our own families. Our own children spent many Christmases at Mozart Avenue before Mom and Dad sold the house. On the last Christmas before Mom and Dad moved into the condo, we all went downstairs for dancing. After dancing to "Daddy," we all gathered in a huge circle in the family room. Dad put on "Auld Lang Syne" played by Tommy Dorsey.

"*For auld lang syne, my jo,*" Dad sang, wrapping an arm around my shoulder. "*For auld lang syne. We'll take a cup of kindness yet.*" He raised his glass, martini splashing my cheek. "*For auld lang syne.*"

14

Mom and Vehicles

One snowy day on my brother's seventeenth birthday, all three of us had a day off school. Duncan headed out with his friend Richard to go skiing in Collingwood. Richard was driving his mother's car. Sandy wanted to go skiing too, so Mom said she would drive Sandy and her best friend, Gail, to the Greyhound bus at Yonge Street and Steeles Avenue. The bus was scheduled to leave at half-past seven that morning, and the depot was only about twenty minutes away. Mom left in my dad's car with Sandy and Gail, telling my father she would be back soon to make his breakfast. Thinking she'd be returning quickly, she set out dressed in her nightgown, Hudson's Bay coat, and boots.

The snow was really coming down, and Mom found the driving more difficult than she had expected. She pulled into the depot just as the bus was pulling out. "Don't worry, girls," she said. "I'll follow it and get the driver to pull over."

My mother was on a mission. She tailgated the bus for miles, but the snow began falling more heavily, and every time she got close enough to pass the bus and make eye contact with the driver, the bus threw up some slush that covered her windshield. She kept going. They passed Highway Seven, Aurora, Alliston, and before she knew it, she was in Barrie.

Mom eventually lost the bus and was about to turn around and go home. Suddenly, however, she saw my brother and Richard at a gas station up ahead. She pulled in and Sandy and Gail tried to wave my brother down, but he simply waved back as Richard drove off. "Don't worry, girls," Mom said. Now Mom set off after Duncan and Richard. This time she caught up with them and they stopped.

"What are you doing in Barrie, Mom?" my brother asked getting out of the car and looking in Mom's car window. "And why are you in your nightgown?"

"It's a long story. Could you fellows take the girls with you to Blue Mountain? They've got their hearts set on going skiing."

"More like Mom's got her heart set on us going skiing," Sandy whispered to Gail.

As Sandy and Gail set out with the boys, Mom turned Dad's car around and headed for home. By now, the snow was falling so heavily she couldn't see two feet in front of the bumper. Nevertheless, she picked up speed. By the time she spotted some vehicles on the shoulder, it was too late. Crash! She smashed Dad's car into a parked truck. There were no cell phones back then, so Mom had no way of contacting my father. A tow truck came and hauled the car back to Toronto. My mother sat beside the driver, her nightgown pulled down over her ankles. The truck pulled into our driveway in late afternoon, not long before my brother and sister returned from their day of skiing. Dad was standing at the front door, still in his pyjamas. I had made him some boiled eggs for breakfast, but he hadn't bothered to get dressed or go to work. He'd been worried sick about my mother, but when she finally walked in, his first words were, "What happened to you? You weren't here to make my breakfast."

"Breakfast?" said my mother. "I haven't eaten a thing all day. I've had a car accident, thank you very much."

"A car accident? In my car?" asked Dad in disbelief.

"Yes, I'm sorry - in your car. I was in Barrie."

"What were you doing in Barrie?" asked my father.

"I took the girls skiing - never mind. I'll tell you later. My neck hurts. The police said I should get it checked out at the hospital. Do you want me to make you some breakfast, first?"

"No, but some soup and a sandwich would be nice."

"Oh, for Christ's sake," said Mom. "Okay. I could eat something, too."

* * *

One Saturday afternoon after the Santa Claus parade, the entire family was returning home in Dad's car when Mom noticed a used car lot on the corner of Dupont and Davenport. "Wow, look at that cute red car." She rolled down her window to get a better look. "Stop, Charlie. It says it's only $500.00."

"Dot, it's a Mercedes Benz," said Dad.

"Exactly. Let's take a look at it."

Dad pulled into the lot and we all got out to assess Mom's dream car.

"I love it, Charlie." Mom hooked her arm through Dad's. "We're never going to get a cheaper price."

My dad looked up to see the dealer coming towards them with his slicked-back brown hair and his bright-yellow-and-green plaid blazer. "It's a bargain, I must admit," said Dad. "Let's take it for a test drive."

"I'll just take you for a spin around the block." The dealer ran to his booth to get the keys.

Duncan was old enough to look after us at that point, so the three of us waited in the lot while Mom and Dad took the car for a drive.

"I hope Mom gets the car," said Duncan.

"Yeah," I said. "She could drive me to my piano lessons."

"And she could drive us to school," said Sandy.

"I get the front seat 'cause I'm the oldest," said Duncan.

"We'll take turns. It's only fair," I said.

"They haven't even bought it yet," said Sandy.

Five minutes later, Mom and Dad returned looking pleased. "We'll take it," said Dad, getting out his cheque book.

"Sure, as long as I can get a look at your driver's licence and take down the number," said the salesman.

"Let's take it home right now, Charlie," said Mom. "The girls can drive with me."

"Yeah!" Sandy and I jumped up and down. "We want to go with Mom."

It was settled. Mom and Dad did the paperwork, and Mom got behind the wheel. I climbed into the front seat, and Sandy got in the back. Dad and Duncan followed us for a while, but once Mom seemed all right on her own, Dad veered off to take the 401.

Mom drove down Avenue Road, through the string of shops and onto York Mills with its hills and exquisite homes. Everything seemed fine. She headed north on Bayview Avenue, with its line of large, lovely homes. She approached Bayview and Sheppard Avenue, one of the busiest intersections in the city, and put on her flicker to turn right onto Sheppard. *Sputter, sputter, spurt, spurt.* The car heaved forward and died.

"What the ...?" Mom turned the key.

"What's wrong, Mom?" I asked.

"I don't know, Jackie," said Mom. "If I knew, I'd fix it."

"Why don't you check the engine?" asked Sandy.

Mom got out and tried in vain to lift up the hood. Cars began to get backed up behind her and started to honk.

"Jesus Christ, shut up," said Mom.

"I thought we weren't allowed to say, 'shut up,'" I said out the passenger window.

"Sorry, dear. I'm just frazzled." The honking increased.

A nice gentleman got out of his car and came to show Mom how to open her hood. Together, they stood looking at the engine.

"I just bought it - not even an hour ago," Mom told the man.

"Huh. Let's check the starter belt." He tinkered around in the engine. "Nope. Seems to be fine. Maybe it's the battery. Let's see. Try it now."

Mom got back behind the wheel and turned the key. Nothing. "Sorry, lady. I can't help you." The man drove off.

Sandy and I sat helplessly in the car. "Dad's not going to like this," I said.

Cars continued to honk at us.

Mom finally stopped a woman in her car and asked if she would kindly call a tow truck for her. The lady agreed. Meanwhile, a CFRB traffic helicopter flew overhead and reported the traffic problem below. Dad was at home listening to CFRB. "A red car is stalled at the corner of Bayview and Sheppard. Traffic is backed up to York Mills. Avoid that intersection." He knew instantly that it was Mom's new Mercedes Benz. The next day, Mom and Dad tried to return the car to the used car dealer. No luck, however. The cars, the booth, the signs – every trace of that business was gone. While the car only cost them $500.00 at the outset, they spent thousands on repairs in the months ahead. It wasn't long before the red Mercedes Benz ended up in a junk heap.

* * *

One night after my graduation, Dad treated the entire family to dinner at the Keg on Leslie Street where I worked as a part-time server while I was at university. There were eight of us for dinner that night. Drinks were flowing - double martinis for Mom and Dad and Keg size Bloody Caesars or beer for the rest of us.

"Let's make a toast to Jackie," said Dad. "Congratulations, on finishing your B.A. and getting on the Dean's List." Dad motioned to the server. "Waiter, we're going to need another round over here."

"*For she's a jolly good fellow,*" Dad sang, getting everyone to join in. "*For she's a jolly good fellow. And none of us can deny.*"

"Mom ended the final chorus with a whoop. "Let's do 'Heart of my Heart.'"

Dad started it off.

"'Heart of my Heart', I love that melody.
'Heart of my Heart' brings back a memory.
When we were kids on the corner of the street.
We were rough 'n ready guys, but oh, how we could harmonize."

The whole family sang along – and loudly. After a few more songs, Dad got up and told one of his shaggy dog tales and we all laughed and laughed.

"Jeez, is your family always this rowdy?" the manager asked me as I headed off to the washroom.

"Yes, I suppose it is," I said smiling. At the time, I thought he must have been envious.

The night wound down. Dad paid the bill and we headed out to the parking lot. Some of us were driving home in Dad's car and Duncan was driving the rest in Mom's car. Duncan was standing with Mom to help her into my father's car, when Dad started to back out.

"Dad! Stop!" yelled Duncan. "You just drove over Mom's foot."

"Oh, yeah - I see the tread mark right there," Mom said, looking down at the tire print on her patent leather shoe. "Didn't feel a thing." I was a bit worried about how much my dad had been drinking, but I got in the back seat and home we went.

* * *

Mom and Dad were visiting their good friends, the Scotts, along with Mary and Jim Baldwin. The Scotts had a lovely home with a very steep driveway. It was a stormy night and the freezing rain was pelting down. Everyone had had a few drinks. When it came time to go home, they headed out to the driveway, treading carefully. Mom slipped and fell flat on her back. Stiff as a board, she slid full speed down the driveway and didn't stop until she was wedged under Dad's car. "Jesus Christ, Dot, what are you doing under there?" asked Dad. "Come out."

"I'm stuck."

"Here, Dot," said Mary. "Give me your hand." The rest of them started to laugh.

"It's not funny," said Dad. "I'm getting soaked out here."

Dad and Donald Scott were both well over six feet tall and strong.

"Here, Charlie," said Donald. "If you and I get down on our knees, I think we can pull her out."

"Okay." Grudgingly, Dad got down on his hands and knees beside Donald. "Dot, give each of us one of your hands."

"Don't hurt me," Mom slid her arms up above her head, so the men could grab her.

"Okay, Charlie. Pull!" Dad and Donald tugged on Mom's arms and out she slithered.

"Look at me - I'm filthy." Mom stared down at her coat, covered with grease. "Thanks, guys."

"Yeah, and now I'm soaking wet," said Dad, looking at his pants.

"Well, sorry," Mom said sarcastically. "Maybe you should have left me there and driven off."

"Oh, Dot," said Dad. "I didn't mean that."

"Let's go," she said. "We're all getting drenched out here." They all carefully tiptoed into their cars and drove home.

* * *

Years later, Mom and a friend organized a weekend trip to Cornwall, Ontario for one of my parents' many curling bonspiels. They rented a mini-bus and a driver. The Beattys joined them, along with the Browns, the Montgomerys, and a few other couples. They all checked into a new hotel near the curling rink. Mom was playing the position of "skip" - the one who aims and throws the granite curling rocks down the ice, toward the bull's eye.

Mom had indulged in a few rye and gingers before the game, and, as she knelt down to thrust the rock forward, her curling glove stuck to the handle. With her hand in her glove and the glove attached to the rock, she was pulled downward straight across the ice. She slid face down in slow motion coming to a full stop about three-quarters of the way down the rink. Her teammates ran to help her. Mom had a good laugh over that one.

Later that night, after several drinks and hours of partying, Mom and Dad tucked into bed. The Beattys were in the room next to Mom and Dad's. John, a practical joker, had brought along a portable record player and a copy of the hit single "I Never Promised you a Rose Garden" - a favourite of his and Dad's. As Dad drifted off to sleep, he heard, "*I beg your pardon, I never promised you a rose garden,*" playing full blast from the room next door. He smiled and rolled over. Three minutes later, he heard, "*I beg your pardon, I never promised you a rose garden. Along with the sunshine, there's gotta be a little rain sometime.*" Then again and again.

"What's John doing?" asked Dad. "I'm going over there." Out the door he went in his pyjamas. He knocked on the Beatty's door.

"Hi, Charlie." John stood in the doorway fully clothed. "What can I do for you?"

"Can you turn down the music, Johnny? We're trying to get some sleep."

"Sure, sure, Charlie boy. Sorry to bother you."

But Dad noticed that John had the record player pushed right up against the wall between the two rooms.

He went back to bed. Five minutes later, he was almost asleep when - "*I beg your pardon. I never promised you a rose garden.*"

"Jesus Christ!"

"Charlie, go give him hell," said Mom.

Dad hammered on the wall with his fist. "Johnny, for Christ's sake. Enough. Dot's trying to sleep."

About thirty minutes went by and Mom and Dad were fast asleep. Then it came another time. Over and over again. They

Mom and Dad's Martinis

put pillows over their heads in a futile attempt to go back to sleep. About an hour later, the music stopped.

On Sunday afternoon, all of the couples climbed into the bus for the ride back to Toronto. The snow was really coming down and the driver had the windshield wipers going full blast. He made a wrong turn somewhere around Brockville.

"Hmm, I'm sure this is the right road," said the driver, barely able to see in front of the windshield.

Everyone in the bus thought it was strange that he was driving down an unplowed country road. On an icy curve, he lost control, went right through a fence, and landed in someone's backyard, just feet from their dining room window. Everyone dragged themselves out of the bus and trudged through the snow into the strangers' home.

"Sorry to bother you," said John Beatty. "We'll pay for your fence."

"Hey, Johnny, why don't you get out your record player and play them that single you brought with you," said Dad. "Play it maybe fifty times." He turned his attention to the owners. "What's for dinner?"

"Oh, Charlie, stop," Mom said, laughing. Everyone else laughed, too, but the owners weren't so sure. My parents and their friends tried to push the bus up the hill, but it was hopeless. A special tow truck for buses had to be called in. Everyone on the bus had to take cabs from the top of the hill. It cost them a fortune to get home.

15

Mom Gets Close

My best friend, Judy, died when I was sixteen years old. She was diagnosed with acute leukemia and died one week later. I scarcely had time to visit her at the Hospital for Sick Children. This once vibrant figure skater and head of the cheerleading squad had suddenly become so pale and weak. Her face and arms were swollen.

"Judy, I'm so sorry," I said.

"Don't be sorry," she said breathlessly. "It's not your fault. I'm happy we got to be friends."

"Me, too," I said. "We've had a lot of fun times together."

"Yeah, we have." She tried to move, but was clearly suffering. "Remember when we had that sleepover at my house, and we snuck out the back, through the sliding doors?" She winced in pain as she laughed.

I nodded. "I love you," I said, trying not to cry.

"I love you, too," she said.

I left her hospital room and went outside to wait for the bus. Tears streamed down my face. Those were her last words to me. I was numb with shock and grief. Mom came with me to the funeral. After that, I went to another friend's house who had a pool. All of Judy's friends who had been at the funeral were there. Everyone was jumping in and out of the water, laughing and having a wonderful time. I couldn't do anything, but think of Judy.

I went home, and spent a few days lying on my bed. Sometimes, I played my guitar. Other times, I just lay there. I eventually came out and sat on the carpet in the living room. I took out my favourite Gordon Lightfoot album and put it on. *"If you could read my mind love, what a tale my thoughts could tell...."* I mouthed along, remembering Judy jumping up and down as a cheerleader. *"And you won't read that book again because the ending's just too hard to take."* I sat there and began to cry inconsolably.

Mom was in the kitchen making dinner. When she heard me weeping, she came into the living room and sat down on the broadloom beside me. I had rarely seen her cry, but for some reason, that day she burst into tears and put her arms around me. "It isn't fair, honey," she said. "It just isn't fair." She gently brushed her fingers through my hair and the two of us sat there, hugging each other and crying.

"But stories always end," Lightfoot sang. *"And if you read between the lines, you'll know that I'm just tryin' to understand."*

It was the closest I had ever felt to my mother. I wouldn't feel that close to her again, until many years later when she became very ill.

16

The Babysitter

Mom and Dad often went away for weekends. One year, they went to Montreal for a few days to visit Dad's old friend and best man, Mike Campbell, and his wife, Laura. Duncan was ten, I was eight, and Sandy was six. They never left us with our regular teenage babysitters for the weekend, and this time, they hired a woman from an agency.

Mrs. Bradley was a tall, thin grey-haired woman without a smile.

On Friday night, she took Duncan, Sandy, and me on a long walk. She led us briskly down Willowdale Avenue, past the hydro field and the row of houses. She kept ahead of us and never looked back to see if we were still with her. It was a late summer afternoon, and we were hot. She bought us some candy and a pop in one store, then told us to wait outside the next.

"You kids can't come in here," she said, grinding out her cigarette with the toe of her heavy brown shoe. "Eat your candy and drink your pop." Minutes later, she came out with a brown paper bag with a few bottles in it. She walked even more quickly on the way back. The moment we got inside the door, she headed for the kitchen and opened a bottle of scotch.

"Go watch TV," she said. "I'll make dinner in a while." Off we went to watch "The Mickey Mouse Club." After about an hour, we came up to the kitchen. Mrs. Bradley had passed out with her head on the table, an empty glass beside her and a lit cigarette in an ashtray.

"Mrs. Bradley," Duncan said. "Mrs. Bradley, when's dinner?" He gave her a shake. "Mrs. Bradley, wake up. We're hungry."

Sandy and I stood watching.

Without even holding up her head, Mrs. Bradley spoke: "Make yourselves a peanut butter and jam sandwich or something. Now leave me alone." She waved us away.

Too frightened to protest, we made ourselves some sandwiches and went back downstairs to watch television. At about midnight, Mrs. Bradley crawled up to my parents' bedroom without even checking on us. After that, the three of us decided to go for a bike ride.

"This is really cool, being out here so late," I said.

"It's not right," said Sandy. "Mom and Dad wouldn't like this one bit."

"Come on, Sandy," said Duncan, popping a wheelie. "Let's just have some fun."

No one came looking for us, so at about one in the morning, we rode home and put ourselves to bed.

On Saturday morning, the three of us got up and went downstairs to watch "The Three Stooges." At about eleven o'clock in the morning, Duncan walked upstairs to wake Mrs. Bradley up.

"Mrs. Bradley - Mrs. Bradley, wake up," he said, touching her shoulder. "We're hungry."

"Oh, for fuck's sake," she said. "Just give me a minute."

"Can we have pancakes?"

"Can't do pancakes, but I'll make youse some French toast. Go make sure there's syrup."

Duncan found the syrup and came back upstairs. "Yep, there's maple syrup. Can we have French toast now?"

"Just a fuckin' minute. I'll have to have some coffee and a cigarette first. Now get outta here."

We went downstairs and continued watching television. After a while, Mrs. Bradley called us.

"Kids, get your butts up here. I made you a decent breakfast."

"Thanks, Mrs. Bradley," I said, as I sat down at the kitchen table with my sister and brother. Mrs. Bradley sat in my mother's chair and lit another cigarette, as she sipped her coffee.

"So, I have a treat for youse guys," she said. "I'm going to take you to see 'Swiss Family Robinson.' We're gonna walk there."

"That's great," said Duncan. "I really want to see that movie."

"Yeah, we love movies," I said.

"So, finish your breakfast and go get dressed."

The walk to the theatre took almost an hour, even with the three of us hurrying along past the Saturday shopping traffic in Mrs. Bradley's wake of smoke. When we got there, Mrs. Bradley read the billboard. "Oh, great, it's a double feature. This is our lucky day."

She bought us popcorn and we went into the theatre and sat down. "Swiss Family Robinson" was fabulous. The whole family lived on a deserted island in the South Pacific. One son had a pet ostrich and the father and mother built a huge tree house where the family lived. I had always wanted a tree house. The second movie was called, "No Man is an Island." It was a true story about World War II when the Americans occupied the Japanese island of Guam. The Japanese invaded and were going around torturing American soldiers and cutting off their heads. It was a horrific film, totally inappropriate for children. Mrs. Bradley seemed to be enjoying it thoroughly, however. I looked over at her and she sat happily eating her popcorn throughout the torture scenes. I had nightmares for years.

After the movie, Mrs. Bradley walked us home, but stopped at the liquor store again. We waited outside while she went in and came out with another bottle in a brown paper bag. She walked us home barely saying a word.

Back at home, Mrs. Bradley said, "Youse guys go play or watch TV or something. I'm gonna have a cigarette and sit here for a while. In a bit, I'll make you the best fuckin' B.L.T.s you ever had. Off you go." We went downstairs to play.

About ninety minutes later, we could smell bacon cooking - a good sign. Soon, however, we saw smoke floating downstairs. The three of us ran up to the kitchen and found a grease fire in the frying pan and no Mrs. Bradley.

"Fire, fire!" Duncan yelled. "Mrs. Bradley, the bacon is on fire!"

I ran over to the sink and got a pot of water and threw it on the fire only to watch it spread across the counter and up the curtains. "Fire, fire!" I screamed.

Sandy ran upstairs to get Mrs. Bradley. She was passed out in my parents' bed with a cigarette burning in the ashtray beside her. "Mrs. Bradley, wake up! The house is on fire!"

"Come on," Duncan yelled. We left Mrs. Bradley in bed and ran outside screaming, "Fire, fire! Our house is on fire!" A neighbour came over while his wife called the fire department. He immediately threw salt on the grease and pulled the curtains down from over the kitchen window and drowned the flames in the sink. The cupboards and ceiling were black with soot. A fire truck arrived a few minutes later and came in to find a house filled with smoke and a drunk lady passed out in my parents' bed.

About two minutes later, the police arrived.

"Who's that lady upstairs?" an officer asked Duncan.

"She's our babysitter. She's weird."

"Where are your parents?" asked the officer.

"They're in Montreal," said Duncan. "They're coming home late tomorrow night."

"Do you have their number? I think they'll want to come home sooner than that."

Duncan found Mom and Dad's number in Montreal and the police officer called them. We listened, as he explained the situation.

"No, they're not hurt. All three are fine. But the babysitter is coming with us down to the station, so they can't stay here alone."

When he hung up, he told us our aunt was coming to pick us up in twenty minutes. Auntie Ruth arrived and helped the three of us pack up overnight bags and sleeping bags. Off we went to our aunt's house where we slept in their family room on the floor with our four cousins. We were quite excited about the overnight.

Mom and Dad didn't pick us up until late Sunday night. It didn't bother me at the time because we got to spend time with our cousins. Years later, however, it seemed strange that they didn't come to get us as soon as possible after what we'd been through.

17

The Dark Times II

When I was twenty-four, I was extremely thin and obsessed with eating as little as possible. One Sunday night, I carefully measured out some canned tuna and green beans on my Weight Watchers weigh scale. Just six ounces of tuna were allowed at dinner. Together with four ounces of green beans, I was going to savour every morsel of that fistful of food on my plate. I gingerly carried the tray downstairs to eat on TV tables in front of the television with my parents, as we did every Sunday night. My parents were eating their typical Sunday night casserole. Duncan sat on the couch, downing his portion. As I placed my precious plate down on the TV table, the whole tray lurched forward and tipped over onto the floor. My sacred tuna was scattered everywhere. There was no more tuna upstairs. I began to sob like a toddler who'd had her favourite toy taken away.

"Oh, Jacelyn, stop it," said Mom. "I'll get you a plate of our casserole while you clean up the mess."

"I can't eat that food." I was down on the floor scooping up pathetic little pieces of tuna and putting them back on my plate.

"Of course you can," Mom said. "It's all food."

"No, it's not," I screamed. "You don't understand. I *can't* eat that food. I *can't*."

"What's wrong with you?" my mother said. "A little bit of chicken and mushroom rice isn't going to kill you. You're skin and bones."

"She's cuckoo," Duncan said matter-of-factly.

"I *CAN'T*." I ran upstairs into my bedroom and slammed the door. I lay on my bed and wailed into my pillow.

"You're making this house a living hell, Jacelyn," Dad yelled up at me.

Sandy was getting married that year. I was upset that my younger sister was settling down while I still had no one. Before the wedding, I tried on my maid of honour dress and looked in the mirror. I didn't like what I saw. I looked fat even though I weighed 105 pounds. I pinched some skin on my waist through the material of the dress to see if I could find any of that deadly fat. I felt about a quarter-inch of skin. I'd have to lose more weight. I looked at my face in the mirror. I didn't know who I was.

One day in March, I decided I was going to commit suicide just like the writer Virginia Woolf did. I thought I would fill my coat pockets with rocks and walk into the frigid waters off Lake Ontario's Woodbine Beach and be done with living. Even though I had a plan, I had second thoughts about carrying it out. I approached my mother in the kitchen.

"Mom, I think I want to kill myself."

She glanced up at me sharply. "Stop that nonsense, Jacelyn."

"No, I'm serious - and I'm scared."

"Look, I've got a tennis game at two." She put on the dishwasher. "I'll get changed and drop you off at Dr. Sherwood's office on my way to the Granite Club. You call his office and tell him you're coming."

She walked down the hall to her bedroom and changed into a white jumper and tennis shoes. I called the doctor's office. I felt like a zombie.

Mom and Dad's Martinis

Mom backed her car out of the garage and opened the passenger door. I got in beside her. We drove all the way to the doctor's office in silence, both of us staring forward. I was filled with a terrible sense of emptiness. She didn't ask me one question about my suicidal thoughts. She pulled into the doctor's parking lot and stopped.

"There you go," she said looking straight ahead.

I got out of the car. "Thank you," I said, feeling a chill run down my spine. I watched as my mother drove off in her whites to play tennis. She didn't even wait to see if I went in.

* * *

I walked into the doctor's waiting room. The sterile smell of disinfectant filled me with fear.

"I'm Jacelyn Cane. I'm here to see Dr. Sherwood."

"Oh, yes, he's expecting you," the nurse said without looking up. "Go down to room two."

I sat on the metal stool in room two. The seat twirled so I twirled with it. Back and forth. Back and forth. Maybe I shouldn't have come. Maybe I could still carry out my plan.

Before long, Dr. Sherwood came in. He stroked his balding black hair, then washed his hands and pulled up a stool beside me. He had been my doctor for a long time. "So, what's going on Jacelyn? Tell me about what's bothering you."

I couldn't look at him. "I feel like I want to kill myself. I hate myself and think it'd be better if I just disappeared."

He took my hand in his. "Do you have thoughts about how you want to do it?"

I told him the details of my plan. "I want to do it today. Nobody wants me around."

"Well, I think it would be good if we got an ambulance to take you over to North York General." He pushed his glasses back, pulled a pen out of the pocket of his white coat and started making some notes. "Is anyone with you? Where's your mother?"

"My mother's playing tennis. I don't want my mother or anyone. I'll go alone."

"Wait here," he said. "We'll let you know when the ambulance arrives. I'll call the hospital and tell them I'm sending you." The ambulance came, and the paramedic accompanied me out of the doctor's office. I was so embarrassed as I walked by the other patients in the waiting room. They could see the ambulance out the window. The paramedic insisted that I lie down on the stretcher. I stared at the ceiling and felt like a fool. At least they didn't run the siren.

We arrived at North York General's Emergency department and the paramedics waited with me for a long time. After several hours of waiting, I was admitted, taken up to the psychiatric unit and placed in an interview room before I was assigned to a bed. A nurse and a psychiatrist came in to see me. The nurse was young with a long brown pony tail. The psychiatrist looked close to retirement with a full head of white hair. Both were dressed casually.

"Tell us what brings you to the hospital today," said the psychiatrist.

"I just feel that everything is hopeless, and there's no point in living," I said. "I feel like I want to die."

"You're very thin," said the nurse. "Are you dieting?" She held my wrist and surveyed the bones pushing up at the surface.

"I don't like eating," I said. "I measure every piece of food that goes into my mouth. Sometimes I eat a lot and then I vomit. One tiny ounce of food makes me feel so fat."

"But you're not fat," said the nurse. "You're extremely thin."

"But I feel obese. I would just like to escape - cease to exist." Just then, I heard my parents' voices out in the hall.

"Where is she?" asked my mother in an angry voice. "I'm her mother and this is her father. We demand to see her right now."

"How did they find out I was here?" I started to cry. "Please, I don't want to see them."

"You don't have to see them if you don't want to," said the nurse. "We'll talk to them."

The psychiatrist stepped into the hallway to talk to my parents.

"I'm sorry," I heard him say. "She's not up to having any visitors right now."

"Don't give me that," said Mom. "I have a right to see my daughter."

"I understand your concerns," said the psychiatrist. "But she doesn't want to see anyone right now. She's an adult, and she has a right to choose. She's been admitted, so you can call tomorrow and see if she wants to see you then."

"Well, this is ridiculous," said Mom. "She'll be lucky if we ever come back."

I heard my parents walk away. Just hearing my mother's voice upset me so much. The doctor gave me something to calm me down.

"Take this," he said. "It will help you relax."

I was feeling pretty mellow the next day when my parents and brother came to visit.

"Well, here you are," said Mom. "I knew it was just a matter of time before you'd end up here."

It was my fault, always my fault.

"I knew you had problems," she went on, "but I also knew you'd have to solve them yourself. You're in the right place."

"Does Sandy know I'm in here? Did you call her in Calgary?"

"I haven't told her yet," said Mom. "She's flying in next week to do some planning for the wedding. We have so many things we have to do. Don't worry. I'll tell her."

Dad and Duncan said hello, but nothing else. They left after a few minutes. I was in the hospital for a month, but neither of them ever came back.

Mom, on the other hand, came to visit regularly, usually at dinner time. "Hi, Jackie. What's on the menu tonight? Let's see," She lifted the lid off my dinner plate. "Yum. Pork chops, mash potatoes and peas. Well, that's a healthy meal." She watched as

I cut tiny pieces of meat and pushed them around on my plate. I ate two at the most and just mushed up the potatoes. I pierced the peas one at a time and ate about five. "What did you have for lunch?" she asked.

"A chicken salad sandwich and soup. What did you do today?"

"Oh, well, let's see. I played tennis with Marcie Conwell and the gang at the club in the morning. We had lunch together there. And in the afternoon, I had a Sanctuary Guild meeting at the church. I'm chairing it now, you know. Then I came here to see you, and now I'm going home to make dinner. Another busy day. I'd better run." She kissed my cheek. "See you tomorrow."

* * *

After two weeks in North York General, my psychiatrist authorized a weekend pass. I felt nervous about going home. Nevertheless, Mom picked me up on the Friday night. The next morning, I found her in the kitchen cooking up a storm.

"Make yourself something for breakfast," she said. "Make sure you tidy up after because we're entertaining tonight, and I want the house spotless."

"What will I do when they're here?" I asked.

"You'll make yourself scarce, that's what," she said, as she stirred the beef bourguignon in the pot on the stove. "I've got a lot to do, so after your breakfast, why don't you go to your room and play your guitar. I'll feed you around five and then you can stay in your room."

"Okay," I said, but I felt sick to my stomach. "Were you able to get the cantaloupe and cottage cheese I asked for?"

"Yes, I did. You're welcome."

"Thanks." I cut a quarter slab out of the cantaloupe and put the rest back in the fridge. I measured a quarter-cup of cottage cheese and scooped it into the centre of the cantaloupe: a perfect breakfast.

Mom cast her eye over my creation. "I still don't understand why you can't just eat what we eat."

"I can't eat regular food like you do because I have a disorder. I've learned that at the hospital."

"I don't have time to talk with you about the hospital."

I ate my cantaloupe and savoured every bite, knowing I was following Weight Watcher's instructions. Afterwards, I cleaned up my dishes and went to my room. After about an hour, I came out. My mother had extended the dining room table and was setting it for ten.

I took a seat in the kitchen. "Can I help?" I asked. I wanted so badly to talk to her about the progress I was making in the hospital.

"No thanks. I've got this." She folded ten white linen napkins and placed them on the matching placemats.

"Can I do the flowers?" I got up and walked over to the vase of pink and white tulips that were waiting to be arranged into a centerpiece.

"No, just leave them," she said. "I like arranging the flowers myself."

I sat back down. "Am I in your way?"

"A little bit, actually."

"Maybe it would be better if I went back to the hospital before your guests arrive," I said after a moment.

Mom stopped what she was doing and looked me straight in the eye. "You know, I think that would be a great idea. No one knows you're in the hospital, and I don't want them to know."

"Well, I might as well go back now then."

"Good idea."

Mom and I drove back to the hospital in silence. Once there, I got out of the car and grabbed my bag and guitar. Tears came as she drove off without saying a word.

* * *

When I was discharged from the hospital after a month, I tried to talk to Mom and Dad about what I had learned. Mom, dressed in dark-green slacks and a light-green blouse, sat in her chair in the family room. Dad sat in his chair in front of the television. "What do you want to talk to us about, Jackie?" He loosened his tie from work. It was an early Friday evening.

"Well," I began. "Sometimes I might have a problem and it would be great if we could sit down with an open mind and talk and listen to one another."

"Okay," said Dad.

"Don't say 'Okay,'" said Mom. "We do a good job of that right now. We're not the problem. You're the one with the problems."

"What do you want to talk about?" asked Dad.

"Well, I'd like to tell you about the skills I learned in the hospital."

"We're not doing that right now," said Mom. "Charlie, make us a martini."

They'd had several drinks by the time I left that night to go to a friend's house.

Mom was upstairs putting the finishing touches on the casserole she was making for dinner.

When I came home a few hours later, they were in the kitchen opening the fridge and looking in the oven.

"Jesus Christ," said Dad. "Where did she hide it?" He looked on top of the fridge.

"I'm home," I said quietly.

Mom whirled around, unsteady on her feet. "Where'd you put my casserole?"

"I didn't put it anywhere," I said. "You were still making it when I went out."

"Don't give us that bullshit, Jackie," said Dad. "You took our casserole, and now we have nothing for dinner."

"This is ridiculous," I said. "Let me look for it." I looked in the oven, in the fridge and on top of the fridge. No casserole. Then

I opened a cupboard door. Sitting on top of the plates was a casserole dish. "Here it is," I said. I took it out and put it in the oven. "I'll put the oven on at 350 for thirty minutes."

"Did you put it in the cupboard?" Dad demanded.

"No, I didn't. This is an absurd conversation." I walked out the front door and went back to my friend's house. When I came home hours later, my parents were already asleep.

* * *

Years after I moved out for good, Ivan and I built our own family: Eliana, Leah, and Victor along with Ivan's daughter Isobel who lived with her mother. Mom and Dad invited the girls to spend a week with them in their rental condo in Florida when Eliana was ten and Leah was seven. It was the first time the two girls had spent a significant length of time alone with their grandparents.

Back in Toronto, the girls told us everything about the drinking in Florida.

"Every night, we were stuck in the bedroom by ourselves while Granny and Grandpa drank martini after martini," Eliana said, as all three of the kids lay on our bed one morning before we got up. Victor, who was only two, was tucked in between Ivan and me.

Leah rolled over to look at Ivan and me. "Grandpa didn't like it if we came out of the bedroom while they were having their before dinner drinks. He would tell us to go back in our room and watch TV."

"You must have been starving," I said.

"We were," said Leah. "Then, on St. Patrick's Day, they took us out to a restaurant for dinner and got really drunk. We were so embarrassed, we hid in the bathroom."

The girls told us that the place was decorated with green shamrocks and streamers and the staff wore green. My parents had several martinis, while the girls drank Shirley Temples. As the band played "When Irish Eyes are Smiling" Mom and Dad sang along: *"When Irish eyes are smiling. Sure, 'tis like the morn in spring. In the lilt of Irish laughter, you can hear the angels sing."*

"Come on girls, sing with us," said Mom.

"We don't know this one, Granny." Eliana twirled her brown curls with her finger: a nervous habit.

"Sure you do, Eli," Mom said. "Grandpa plays this song all the time."

Mom and Dad kept ordering drinks and soon they were on their feet dancing and singing. The girls took the chance to slip off and go to the washroom together.

"I'm so embarrassed," said Eliana.

"Me, too." Leah combed her blonde ringlets.

"Let's just hang out in here for a while," said Eliana.

"They must have had five martinis already - not to mention the ones at home."

"How's Grandpa going to be able to drive?"

"Maybe we'll take a taxi and get the car tomorrow," said Leah.

"I doubt it."

The girls waited in the washroom until their grandmother came stumbling in.

"Here you are," said Mom. "We were worried about you. Come on out. You're missing all the fun."

It was another hour before Dad drove everyone home, barely able to walk let alone drive.

Ivan listened to the whole story, then turned to me. "We shouldn't have let them go, Jackie."

"I know. I'm really sorry. I feel horrible about it. Believe me. It'll be the last time any of you are left alone with Granny or Grandpa."

* * *

Mom and Dad were still enjoying their holiday in Florida when I received a phone call from Sandy.

"I'm sorry to tell you this, Jackie, but our dear grandmother Clarke died last night."

"Oh, no, poor Grandpa. How's he doing?"

"Auntie Rose said he had a very difficult time getting to the hospital last night. He was distraught."

"She was ninety-four," I said. "They were married for more than sixty-five years. What will he do without her?

"It'll be really hard for him, I'm sure," said Sandy.

"Did she die from the anaesthetic?"

"Apparently, yes. It had a horrible effect on her kidneys and heart."

We talked a little longer, then I said, "I'm going to call Dad in Florida. They'll have to come home."

While my dad's sister and brother began making the funeral arrangements, I called my parents in Florida.

"Yes, I know Granny died," said Dad. "But we're not coming home for the funeral."

"You have to come home," I said. "It's your mother's funeral."

"We don't have to do anything." Mom had picked up the bedroom phone. "We have two more weeks of holiday that we've already paid for."

"Grandpa needs you," I said. "He's heartbroken."

"Jackie, he'll be fine, said Dad. "We'll spend time with him once we're back. It's only two more weeks."

I felt numb. "Couldn't you just fly in for the day?"

After Sandy and Duncan had made similar calls to pressure my parents, they finally agreed.

Tall and lean, Grandpa stood by Granny's open casket as my parents arrived just in time for the funeral.

"Hi, Pop." Mom hugged Grandpa and kissed him on the cheek. "I'm so sorry about Mom. She was a wonderful woman."

"Hi, Dad," said my father. "Mom lived a good life. You had many happy years together."

Those were the only words my parents spoke to my grandfather at the funeral or the reception.

"Aren't you going to sit beside Grandpa?" I asked Dad.

"Uncle Albert is there," he said.

"But you're the oldest. You should sit with him."

"Relax, Jackie. It's fine."

I felt such resentment towards my parents. Then they were on the earliest plane back to Florida the next morning.

* * *

Years passed, and our wonderful Grandpa Cane died at the age of one hundred. Again, Mom and Dad happened to be at their rented condominium in Florida. And no, they weren't coming home for the funeral.

"Jackie, Grandpa's gone now," Mom said over the phone. "We'll have a memorial for him when we get home. Go ahead and have the funeral."

"It's a matter of respect," I said, "for a man we all loved."

"As I just said," she continued. "We'll show respect and celebrate his life when we return. Grandpa won't know if we're there or not."

"We'll know. Auntie Rose and Uncle Albert will know."

"Don't worry. We'll call them and explain."

Sandy and I got together with our Auntie Rose. Together, we planned the funeral with her daughters and the minister at Grace Church on-the-Hill.

On the day, Sandy spoke for our family.

Sandy looked pale and drawn in the soft-grey sweater set she had received from my grandmother. She gripped the podium and took a breath. "I remember the first time Granny and Grandpa went to McDonald's. There they were, a couple that was used to fine dining and the best service this city had to offer. Together, they sat at a table and waited. 'Terrible service in this place, Jane,'

Grandpa said to Granny. They eventually got up and left. They told all of us to avoid the place."

I had written a song about my grandparents. I stood on the dais with my guitar and sang,

"Here's to the grandparents who gave me so much.
Oh, how I love you so.
I'll hold you forever in my heart.
And I wish you didn't have to go."

It felt so strange not to have my parents present. My children wondered why they weren't there. Nobody understood their thinking.

Weeks later at the memorial, Mom got really upset when I sang the song again.

"It was a tribute to Granny and Grandpa," I said. "I had every right to sing it. Besides, Auntie Rose asked me to."

She glared at me. "It made people too sad," she said.

* * *

When Eliana was twelve, Leah was nine and Victor was four, Ivan and I built a large deck on the back of our house. We decided to invite my parents over for dinner. Ivan cooked a beautiful salmon, and we provided a nice tray of cheese and crackers for an hors d'oeuvre. I had made a frozen, whipped orange sherbet for dessert. It was a perfect summer night and we all sat out on the deck for cocktails. Ivan and I had a couple of rum and Cokes, but Mom and Dad were really dipping into the gin.

"The deck is great, just great," Mom slurred from her deck chair.

"Yeah, they really did a good job," said Dad. "Dot, ready for another drink?" He shook his empty glass in her face.

"Sure am, Charlie."

Dad went into the kitchen and poured them another.

"Yeah, we're very pleased with it," I said. I went into the house to check on the beans. The gin bottle was about three-quarters empty.

"Everything's ready," I called, putting a bottle of white wine on the table.

"Yep, the salmon is ready too." Ivan brought the tray into the kitchen. We served the meal on my grandmother's fine china.

"Mom and Dad, you come and sit here." I helped my mom into her seat. "Kids, you sit on the other side."

"I'll just pour us one last martini to have with dinner," Dad said, heading for the kitchen.

"Oh, we have wine, Dad. It's okay."

"No, no," he said. "We'll have both."

I felt a knot in my stomach. I poured them both a little bit of wine and Dad brought out the martinis. We all sat down to eat.

"So kids, how's school?" Mom asked, as she ate.

"We're on summer holidays, now," said Eliana.

"Yeah, I'm going to camp," said Leah.

"Oh, that's right," said Mom.

"And then we're going to the cottage," said Victor.

"Oh, that'll be fun," said Dad.

"I'll have more wine, Ivan," said Mom. A chunk of salmon fell off her fork into her lap.

"Are you sure, you're okay?" I asked. "You've already had a lot to drink."

"I'm fine." She reached for the wine bottle and poured more wine for herself and Dad.

They both ate a bit more and then Mom buckled over from the waist and her head landed right in her salmon. She was out cold. I looked at Dad. Chair and all, he had leaned back against the deck rails and passed out.

I tried shaking them. "Mom, Dad, wake up."

The three kids looked on in shock. "Are we still having dessert?" Victor asked after a moment.

"Yes, we're having dessert. I'm so sorry, kids." I lifted my Mom's head off her plate, took away her dish and laid her head back down on the table-cloth.

"They definitely drank too much," said Eliana.

"Honestly, Jackie, this is disgusting," said Ivan.

"I agree," I said. "They're like children - no wait; that's an insult to our children."

We cleared the table, and the five of us ate dessert as though nothing had happened. Eventually, we were able to rouse them enough to get them in a taxi and send them home.

Dad called the next morning and was furious that his car wasn't there.

"Dad, you'd had way too much to drink," I said. "You couldn't possibly have driven home."

"I do it all the time," he said. "Now bring my car up here right now. I need it."

Ivan drove Dad's car, and I followed him in our car. Ivan came into their condo with me to give my dad his keys.

"Here they are, Dad." I placed the keys on the front hall table.

"I had planned to go to the Granite Club this morning and Mom's out. It really threw off my day."

"Dad, you were plastered last night. You passed out. You could've killed someone or yourselves if we'd let you drive home."

"Enough of that. I drive home from parties all the time."

"We gave the taxi driver sixty dollars for the trip home," said Ivan.

"Well, that was your choice, not mine," said Dad. "Anyways, I'm off to the club."

"God," said Ivan as we walked to our car. "It's a miracle your father hasn't killed someone by now."

"I know," I said, as I got in the car. "And he was so abusive."

That was the last time we ever invited my parents to dinner on their own.

18

The Parties

Mom and Dad were very social beings. There were gatherings every weekend: sometimes, at our house, sometimes, elsewhere, but they were always going to parties.

One year, they had their friends Mary and Jim Baldwin up to our rental cottage in Muskoka for the weekend. On Saturday night, they headed off to a party in Dad's inboard motor boat. We children were eleven, thirteen, and, fifteen by then, so we didn't need a babysitter. We waved them off.

"Night, Mom. Night, Dad." I untied the boat and pushed them off.

"Don't wait up," Dad said, as he slowly backed away from the dock. "We'll be home about one." Dad looked sharp in a turquoise shirt and beige pants. Balding Jim sat beside him in the front. Mom and Mary sat in the back. Mary's black-rimmed glasses where pushed back on top of her grey hair, cut short as usual. Mary was wearing a regal-blue silk shirt over her white pants. Mom was also wearing white pants with a sleeveless yellow-and-pink plaid blouse. Mom and Dad were drinking martinis out of red plastic cups. Mary was drinking scotch.

"Mary, can you get me a beer?" said Jim.

"Sure." Mary reached into the cooler and grabbed a bottle of Labatt's Blue. She used the opener tied to the handle of the cooler. "Here, hon."

Duncan and Sandy and I played Monopoly, and, before we knew it, it was one o'clock. No Mom and Dad. An hour or so passed. Still, no parents.

"I'm worried," Sandy said, as she put away the Monopoly money.

"I am, too." I paced in front of the fireplace.

"I hope they didn't have an accident," said Duncan, as he lay down on the couch. In the city, we were used to Mom and Dad staying out until all hours, but somehow, when they were out in a boat, it was different.

It was four o'clock when we heard Dad's voice off in the distance: "Stroke, stroke, stroke." Then we heard laughter coming from the others.

We saw the navigation lights reflected in the moonlit water as the boat came around the corner. Mom was steering, but the engine was silent. Mary was sitting beside her, drinking out of her plastic cup. Dad was in the back, paddling with a paddle. Jim was on the other side paddling with the lid of a cooler.

"We're almost there, Jimmy. Just a few more strokes," said Dad. "Christ, Dot, steer us to the dock."

"What happened?" Duncan yelled.

"We ran out of gas way back near the O'Keefe's cottage," said Dad.

"Why are you guys still up?" Mom asked, slurring.

"We were really worried." Sandy grabbed the rope Mom threw to her and tied up the boat. Mom was first out. She stumbled onto the dock and almost fell in the lake.

"Oopsy."

"Watch it, Dot," said Mary, laughing.

"Oh, nothing to worry about," said Jim. "We had it under control." He held up the lid of the cooler. "Always remember to take two paddles, though." All four of them stumbled up to the cottage and went to bed.

* * *

When we got older and had boyfriends and girlfriends or spouses of our own, the Baldwins started inviting us all up to their cottage on Georgian Bay every Canada Day weekend. In 1983, we arrived with eight people. The Baldwin's cottage was a quaint old log cabin with a wonderful loft where extra bodies slept in sleeping bags on the floor. It was the first time my live-in boyfriend (later husband), Ivan, met my family. Ivan slept in the loft which, while cozy, had bats flying around in it. I slept on a couch in the screened-in porch. Sandy and her husband, John slept on a pullout couch together because they were married. My brother, Duncan and his wife, Liz got to sleep in a bedroom. Of course, Mom and Dad did, too.

Every night of the weekend began with cocktail hour out on the Baldwin's deck. Mom and Mary served beautiful trays of cheese and crackers, and it was martini time for my parents. The Baldwins drank scotch. Then, we all gathered for a beautiful sit-down dinner in the screened-in dining porch. Dad and Jim cooked steaks to perfection outside on the barbecue, drinks in hand. While flipping a sirloin steak and sipping his martini, Dad said, "Jimmy, if I felt any better, I'd have to call a doctor." This was a classic line my dad often repeated while diving into martini time.

Mom and Mary were inside getting the green beans and creamed cauliflower ready. Soon, we all sat down to eat.

"I'd like to make a toast," said Ivan. "A toast to all of you. I'm happy to feel so welcomed into your family."

"Aw, that's so nice of you to say," said Sandy. "We're so glad you could join us."

Mom had drunk a few too many martinis. With every spoonful of cauliflower, she served onto a plate, she took a spoonful of creamed sauce and slurped it up. "Sho good," she said, as sauce oozed down her chin. "Sho good. Sho good."

"Dot, stop that," said Dad. "Just serve the vegetables."

The rest of us were laughing uncontrollably. I had warned Ivan about my parents' drinking, and now he was witnessing it first-hand. To this day, we imitate that moment every time someone says something is "so good."

"Sho good," we joke. "Sho good."

After dinner, we all headed out onto the large deck overlooking the water. Dad brought out his ukulele, and I took out my guitar. We sang for hours. I led them in a layered round of "The Lion Sleeps Tonight," while Dad insisted on taking the highest part and projecting his beautiful baritone voice into a falsetto that pierced the night. He was really enjoying himself. Then I played Joni Mitchell's "Carrie," and everyone joined in on the chorus.

"Charlie, play 'Personal Friend of Mine,'" Jim urged.

Dad grinned and strummed the opening chord. He sang that song several times, slowing it down and then picking up the pace. He kept the ending going for twenty minutes or more.

Around four o'clock in the morning, the party broke up and we all made our way to bed. We started in again the next morning. Sandy was pregnant with her first child and wasn't drinking. "I drank when I was pregnant with you, and you turned out all right," Mom said. "You could at least have a Bloody Caesar this morning."

My sister refused.

As the weekend came to an end, Mom and Dad were the first to head back to Toronto. The rest of us gathered on the deck to have a burger before we hit the road. "We'd all better watch out for Pierre Trudeau," said Jim. "He's turning this country towards socialism." Jim had amassed a small fortune and was on his way to becoming a very rich man. "I don't agree with this universal health care bullshit. Why should I be paying for someone else to go to the doctor when I can buy the best doctors in the world?"

We never talked about politics in my house growing up; nevertheless, I spoke up.

"Do you want us to be like Chile where everyone has to bring their own sheets to the hospital?"

Ivan had come to Canada in 1974 as a Chilean refugee after the military coup led by Pinochet. Chile had moved from socialism to fascism overnight. I had listened to Jim and Mary Baldwin spout their increasingly right-wing views for years, and I had reached the boiling point.

"Don't come here and shoot off your mouth with your political views, Jacelyn," said Mary. "Get out, now."

"This whole weekend has been political," I said. "Come on, Ivan. Let's go." Our bags were already packed, so Ivan and I were able to make a quick get-away. As we ran to my car, Mary burst through the bushes to confront me. It was like a scene out of the movie, "The Blair Witch Project."

Mary dug her long nails into my arm. "Don't you ever come back here and talk like that again. *Ever.*"

"Hey, Jackie," Jim called out from the deck. "I love your independent spirit. Keep it up."

Ivan and I tried to deconstruct the events all the way to Toronto.

When we got home, he shook out his towel only to have two bats fly out and circle our bedroom. "That one's Mary and the other is Jim," said Ivan.

My mother phoned shortly thereafter, having received a call from Mary. "How dare you contradict the Baldwins when you were guests at their cottage," she said. "You couldn't have been ruder if you had tried."

"They couldn't have been more obnoxious," I said.

"Don't ever talk like that again - that is, if you're ever lucky enough to be invited back."

Mom and Dad's Martinis

As so often happened when my mother and I had a difference of opinion, one of us hung up on the other. We went for weeks without speaking.

* * *

The Baldwins weren't my parents' only friends with a cottage on Georgian Bay. Mom and Dad visited their friends Artie and Shirley Mackenzie every summer at their cottage in Pointe au Baril. The Mackenzie's and John and Joan Beatty were cottage neighbours. Every summer, the three couples, along with others, boarded the Beatty's lobster trawler and made their way through the rocky, and at times treacherous, waters around Pointe au Baril to Paul and Betty Barry's island cottage in the open waters of Georgian Bay.

The Barrys hosted an annual costume party with a British monarchist theme. Artie Mackenzie always dressed as one of the Queen's Buckingham Palace Foot Guards – complete with an official red tunic, black pants, and a tall bearskin hat with a gold chin strap. He stood at attention in the back of the boat and saluted anyone who passed. Shirley often dressed as Queen Elizabeth with a necklace from a thrift shop and a crown made out of aluminum foil with fake jewels glued to it. Of course, all of the women wore white gloves. Some men dressed as aristocrats and others dressed as Beefeaters, the Tower of London guards.

"After you, your Royal Highness," said Artie, as he helped Shirley off the boat.

"Kind sir, don't touch my garments," said Shirley. "It's against protocol. Just get me a gin and tonic."

"As you wish, your Majesty."

Dad dressed as King Henry VIII and Mom dressed as Ann Boleyn ready to have her head chopped off. Dad wore a fake beard and a flat hat with a white feather in it. He had bought a large woman's dress, cut it off above the knees and puffed up the sleeves with tissue paper. White tights and slippers completed the look, along with the large gold necklace he draped around his shoulders as his chain of office. Mom wore a floor-length gown with an empire waist. She had her hair parted in the middle and flattened back under a black scarf that draped down her back. She had glued two fake strings of pearls to the scarf.

"Come along, Anne, come along. Don't dawdle," my father said. I think it was one of the only times he got away with bossing Mom around.

When the party was over at about three in the morning, the Mackenzies, the Beattys, and my parents toppled into the lobster trawler and headed for home. There was a thick fog and they had all had a lot to drink.

"Where is that southern shore?" asked John. "It's usually right about here." He was driving slowly and steering clear of some rocks. "I think we turn down here."

"No, Johnny. I think we go left, over there," said Artie, who usually knew the waters well.

Before they knew it, John was steering into a boathouse.

"Are we home, Johnny?" asked Dad. "This doesn't look familiar."

"Not sure, Charlie," said John. "Just let me check."

They were in a stranger's boathouse, far away from home. John backed the boat out. With everyone still dressed in full monarchist regalia, he carefully made his way home, dropping Mom and Dad and the Mackenzies off on the way.

The following night, the Beattys joined Mom and Dad at the Mackenzie's for a game of cards. A huge thunder-storm came up. Lightning struck the Mackenzie's sleeping cabin and set it on fire. Everyone went running with water to put out the fire - with the exception of Dad who ran and changed out of his crisp white pants before going near the fire. The sleeping cabin burned to the ground, but no one was hurt, and the fire didn't spread. When they went back into the main cottage, they noticed all the photographs on the wall had been turned to negatives because of the lightning.

Mom and Dad's Martinis

"Wow, look at these photos of the kids," said Shirley. "Sam and Don have black faces and white hair."

"The cottage is white," said Mom.

"Hey, Charlie. Are your white pants clean?" said Artie. "They didn't get dirty in the fire, did they?"

"Wouldn't want that to happen," said John. The group razzed my Dad about his decision to change out of his good pants. This went on for the rest of the night and for years to follow.

* * *

The Beattys had costume parties, but of a slightly different nature. In the morning, Joan gave everyone a brown paper bag containing a prop. They had the rest of the day to create a well-known character and be prepared to act out a short skit. One year, Mom got a bag with a French beret in it, and Dad got an orange mop head. The Beattys had five daughters, so they had a marvelous costume chest. Mom found herself some white face makeup and a black-and-white striped T-shirt, and dressed up as Marcel Marceau. She used her own eyeliner to paint eyebrows on her forehead and put together a wonderful mime show to perform for the other guests.

Dad used his mop head to dress up like Lucille Ball in "I Love Lucy." He used bobby pins to curl some of the mop strands into curls around his forehead. Then he tied the rest back into a ponytail and covered his head with a red kerchief. He found an apron and a polka-dot dress. He wore a pair of flats and carried a mixer bowl and a spoon. He finished his costume off with some bright red lipstick and black mascara.

When it came time for his skit, he gave John Beatty a piece of burnt toast.

"Ricky, I didn't mean to burn your toast. Here let me scrape it off for you." He scraped the burnt layer of toast into John's lap.

* * *

Mom, Shirley Mackenzie, and Joan Beatty all had their fiftieth birthdays during the same summer, so the Mackenzies hosted a huge party for all three. I was working as a newspaper reporter at the Winnipeg Tribune at the time, but I flew in to surprise Mom. I hid under the deck of the boat as it pulled up to the cottage, then jumped up at the last moment.

"It's Jackie. It's *you*, Jackie," Mom said, as we hugged and soaked up the moment of surprise.

"When did you fly in?"

"Last night."

"What a wonderful treat. Now the whole family's here. Let the party begin."

And party she did. Someone gave her a pair of gold tap shoes. She put them on and jumped up on the pine dining room table. Dad grabbed his ukulele. He played "In a Shanty in Old Shanty Town." It was often sung by crooners, but Dad picked up the pace, so my mother could do her thing in her tap shoes.

"It's only a shanty in old Shanty Town.
The roof is so slanty it touches the ground.
But my tumbled down shack by an old railroad track,
like a millionaire's mansion is calling me back."

Mom tapped and danced and twirled until she practically fell off the table. I watched my mother hoofing it in her tap shoes on top of the pine table and wondered how old she was. She was behaving like an eighteen-year-old. Wasn't I supposed to be the child? Or at least the young woman? After Mom's dancing, everyone sang together for hours. Mom kept her tap shoes on for the rest of the party.

* * *

Mom and Dad's Martinis

One summer, Mom and Dad rented a cottage on the Ojibway Island in Pointe au Baril with their friends Harry and Susan Beam. It was the weekend of the Ojibway Regatta and Mom and Dad decided to enter the canoeing foursomes' race along with Pam Smith and Harry Beam. All four were large people at that time. Standing on the dock, Dad pulled the canoe up to the edge so they could get into it. First, Mom got in at the bow. Then, Pam Smith and Harry Beam got in the middle and all three laid their paddles across the gunnels ready to paddle out to the starting line. Dad got in last. As soon as he sat down in the stern, everyone heard *glug, glug, glug*. The canoe slowly sank. Mom and Dad and the other two laughed hysterically as their foursome disappeared beneath the surface and slowly tipped over.

"Come on, Charlie," said John Beatty from the viewer's dock. "Steer you team."

"Don't give up now," said Artie Mackenzie, as he stood beside John. "You can do it." There was a large crowd gathered and everyone was enjoying the moment.

I stood on the viewers' dock with Sandy and Duncan and the other kids our age, laughing at our drenched parents. The regatta organizers helped Mom and Dad and the others out of the water and retrieved their canoe before awarding them the booby prize.

* * *

Dad's best man at his wedding was Mike Campbell, whom he'd met while working in Montreal. Though Mike and his wife, Laura continued to live in Quebec, they rented a cottage in Pointe au Baril one summer, too. They invited Mom and Dad for the weekend along with a few other couples. As was the case with many Pointe au Baril cottages, the one they rented was very large and rickety, and each room had its own balcony. The cottage was three stories and slept eighteen people. Mom and Dad had been up until around three in the morning playing cards with the Campbells and the other guests.

"I've got a full house." Mike brushed his plump hand through his full head of hair and removed his glasses, placing the earpiece in his mouth for dramatic affect.

"I call your bluff," said Mom. She laughed, as she realized he had the cards.

Eventually everyone headed off to their bedrooms. Mom and Dad were right beside the Campbells.

At about four in the morning, Laura knocked on Mom and Dad's bedroom door.

"Charlie, sorry to bother you." She was much shorter than Dad. Her grey hair was brushed back, and she was dressed in a pink housecoat. "Mike went to the washroom about half an hour ago, and now he's gone. I'm worried he may have fallen on the rocks or something. Could you look around the cottage for him - and outside too?"

Dad was barely awake. "Okay, okay. I'll take a look." He grabbed a flashlight.

Mom rolled over and went back to sleep, as Dad went off searching for Mike. About ten minutes later, a man came into Mom's bedroom, climbed into bed beside her and went to sleep.

Dad held up his flashlight surveying the rocky shore, but Mike was nowhere to be found. Dad went back inside and searched throughout the cottage. There were a lot of empty bedrooms to look in. No Mike. He must be back in bed by now, Dad thought. He gave up and went back to bed. He crawled in and went to sleep. About fifteen minutes later, he woke up and realized he had his arms around another man.

"What the …?" said Dad. "Mike, what are you doing in here? Why are you in bed with my wife?"

"*Your* wife?" said Mike. "Where's Laura?"

"You're in our bedroom, Mike, and Laura is worried sick about you. Your bedroom is next door."

Mom and Dad's Martinis

"Sorry, Charlie. I'll go now," said Mike.

Having had her fill of martinis and other cocktails, Mom slept through it all.

* * *

Mom threw Dad a surprise party for his fortieth birthday. There were about thirty people gathered at our old house on Silverview Drive in Willowdale. Dad had been curling after work and was expected home late. It was Duncan's job to put out the garbage every week and he'd returned the bins to the garage after collection as he was supposed to. However, a friend of Dad's, Donald Scott, thought it would be funny to play a trick on my father. He took the two garbage cans and placed them at the end of the driveway, so Dad couldn't get his car in the garage. When Dad arrived, he got out of the car and put the bins back in the garage, cursing my brother all the way. When Dad walked in the house, he yelled out, "Duncan, get down here."

Everyone screamed, "Surprise!" as Duncan jumped out of bed and ran downstairs.

"Oh, my God," said Dad, as he surveyed the large group of people gathered in the living room. "Duncan, never mind. I'll talk to you tomorrow."

"No need to take it out on him, Charlie," said Donald. "I'm the one who put your garbage cans at the end of the driveway." Mom and the other guests gathered around Dad and laughed.

"Oh, for Christ's sake, Don," said Dad. "Now I'm embarrassed."

"That was the goal, Charlie," said Donald. "That was the goal."

"Dot, can you get me a drink?" said Dad. That was when he noticed Duncan still standing in his pyjamas. "Duncan, why don't you go back to bed?"

* * *

Mom and Dad celebrated their fortieth anniversary with a huge party at the Granite Club. It took place in the ballroom with its exquisite chandeliers, oak floor, and stage. Tables were set all around the room with white linen tablecloths and purple and pink rose centrepieces. About seventy people were present. Sandy, Duncan, and I made a speech for our parents.

"Mom and Dad, you have taught us the importance of friendship," said Sandy. "You have many friends you've had since your childhoods, and not many people can say that anymore. And you have friends you've made over the years. You treat them all like they mean so much to you because they do."

"Mom and Dad, you sure know how to have a good time," said Duncan. "There are so many funny stories - I'll share just a few now. Mom, remember how you set out to drive Sandy to her ski bus just twenty minutes away and came back eight hours later having driven Dad's car into a ditch outside Barrie? Meanwhile, Dad was upset that you weren't there to cook his breakfast. Then there was the foursome canoe race in Pointe au Baril. You ended up at the bottom of the lake and won the booby prize." The guests erupted in laughter.

When it was my turn, I stepped forward and took the podium. "As parents, you have taught us the importance of family," I said. "Mom, you were never one to carry a broom in your hand - unless it was a curling broom that is. But, both you and Dad were always home for dinner - and expected us to be there too. We've been so lucky to have a great extended family, as well."

Dad's parents were present, so Dad gave a tribute to them, too. There was a band, and we danced to jazz hits from the 1950s in honour of Mom and Dad. Guests jigged and jittered to "Have You Met Miss Jones?" and "One O'clock Jump."

Twenty years later, Mom and Dad celebrated their sixtieth anniversary in a smaller room at the Granite Club, but they still invited about sixty guests. This time, the grandchildren provided some of the entertainment. Ivan and I looked on with pride as our children, Eliana, Leah, and Victor, sang "Yellow Bird" with harmony while Leah played the ukulele. Sandy's two children, Robbie and Annie, made a toast to their grandparents. Duncan made a speech and Sandy read a poem she'd written that highlighted their zest for life.

To round off the show, I led a singsong with song sheets and my guitar. Everyone sang a few rounds of "The Lion Sleeps Tonight" and other songs. Mom and Dad and all the guests took part.

"Aren't they great kids?" Mom whispered to The Reverend Dr. Andrew Lawson, who was seated beside her at dinner.

"Yes, they're all terrific," he said.

Dad's dementia had been getting worse for some time.

"I want to go home now," he said, as soon as dinner was finished.

"Oh, Charlie, stop it," said Mom. "The kids haven't even performed yet."

"I'm tired," Dad said again after Sandy read her poem. "Can we go now?"

"No, Charlie. We haven't heard from the grandchildren yet," said Mom.

The performances came to an end with the singalong, and Dad spoke up again.

"I want to go home now, Dot."

"Dry up, Charlie. We're not leaving until our guests leave." Mom got up and mingled with people while Dad sat at his seat and waited. He didn't speak to anyone. He was just counting the minutes until he could leave. The party wound down around ten.

* * *

One of the perks of being President of the Granite Club was that a President's Ball was held in Mom's honour. It was a big deal. Mom offered to buy new dresses for Sandy and me and my brother's wife, Liz. It was the only time in his life that Ivan wore a tux. Somehow, Mom didn't trust my ability to buy my own dress, so she took me shopping. She dragged me through stores like Holt Renfrew and The Bay, where I wouldn't normally shop, and had me trying on some of the most inappropriate dresses, including a shocking pink strapless number with sequins all over it. The hem was about eight inches above my knees.

"Oh, that's gorgeous, Jackie," said Mom, as I reluctantly stepped out of the change room. "It really highlights your figure."

"It's not me, Mom. I don't dress like this, and you know it," I said. "I want to go to Red Emma's. I love the dresses there. And they're all handmade."

"Okay, I give up," said Mom. At Red Emma's on Queen Street West, I picked out what I thought was a lovely mauve dress with a hand painted detail down the side of it. Mom looked me up and down. "I wouldn't be caught dead in that thing, but whatever floats your boat."

At about eleven o'clock in the morning on the day of the President's Ball, I got a call from Mom.

"We're in Emergency," she said. "We've been here since three a.m. Dad's heart is fibrillating again, damn it."

"Is he okay?" I asked.

"He's going to be fine. This always happens when he's stressed."

"Or when he drinks too much," I said.

"That's not the problem. Honestly, I swear he's trying to sabotage my party."

"That's ridiculous, Mom. Don't say that. He's sick. He needs a pacemaker like the doctors have been telling you."

"Well, we're not dealing with that today. I have a hair appointment in a few hours."

I took a deep breath. "Dad may be too sick to go tonight."

"Oh, he's definitely going," said Mom defiantly. "And he'll be standing in that receiving line. No one in a wheelchair is going to be at my side."

"Mom, that's terrible."

Sure enough, limousines picked up each member of the Cane family and Dad was standing in the receiving line in his tuxedo that night. In every photograph of my dad at that ball, his face is grey.

* * *

Mom and Dad threw a beautiful party at Mozart Avenue for my Cane grandparents' fiftieth wedding anniversary. Mom cooked all the food for the fifty guests and hired waiters to tend bar, serve hors d'oeuvres, and help serve dinner. My grandmother wore a corsage and my grandfather had a boutonniere. Mom knew how to throw a good party.

Dad made a wonderful speech about my grandparents.

"Mom, Dad, you've been a rock for our family all these years," said Dad. "Your love for one another shines through every day, and your marriage is a wonderful example to all of us about the importance of commitment, friendship, and fun."

After dinner, it was time for dancing. Dad played records from the twenties to honour my grandparents and their wedding. He played "Sweet Georgia Brown" and "Dinah." When he put on "Bye, Bye Blackbird," my grandfather and I danced a bit of the Charleston together. After a few verses, I let my grandmother cut in. It was a wonderful party. Too much champagne, however. I had a terrible hangover the next day.

* * *

Ivan and I got married at Mom and Dad's house in the middle of winter. There were one hundred guests. Again, Mom cooked all the food except for the wedding cake and other desserts, and waiters and bartenders were brought in to help out. As flower girl, Ivan's daughter, Isobel, had to walk down my parents' huge staircase first, followed by Sandy, my matron of honour. I descended last, with Dad at my side. Ivan and I said our vows against the snowy backdrop of my parents' family room window. Purple heather and tulips were draped over lit candelabra that stood before the frosty view of the ravine out back. Ivan and I had written our own vows. We said them in English, but he also did a couple of readings in Spanish for the many Spanish-speaking guests.

"He's not going to speak in Spanish, is he?" my mother asked with exasperation. She kept sighing loudly as Ivan read. "Is he done yet?"

I could feel my cheeks turning red. I gave her a dirty look, but said nothing.

After the ceremony, everyone sat down all over the house to eat dinner. I had invited Isobel's mother, Loretta, so she could see her daughter as flower girl. She was also a friend. Mom sat down beside her not knowing who she was. "I'm Dorothy Cane," said Mom.

"I'm Loretta O'Laney - Isobel's mother."

"Oh, Isobel is such an easy-going child. It's always a pleasure to have her with us," said Mom. "Jacelyn, on the other hand, now, she was a difficult child."

When I found out about that conversation weeks later, I called my mother to confront her about it.

"Well, you were a difficult child - that's all there is to it," Mom said.

I remembered all the times my mother ignored me when I needed to talk. "And you were a difficult mother." With that, I hung up the phone. Again, it was weeks before we spoke.

At the wedding, dinner came to an end and the dancing began. Ivan and I had put together several mixed tapes that would please everyone. There was plenty of Frank Sinatra, Benny Goodman, and Tommy Dorsey for my parents and their friends. For us, we had Carlos Puebla from Cuba and Violeta Parra from Chile. It was humorous to see Mom and Dad's friends dancing to the Latin beat as Carlos Puebla sang in Spanish about agrarian reform in Cuba. None of them had a clue. Then "Free Nelson Mandela," came on - a wonderfully upbeat, but very political song. Again, everyone got up and danced.

Mom's father was at home that night and very ill with cancer. At about midnight, Mom got a call from her stepmother, Dolores, to say he had just died. I felt so badly for my mother who had just prepared this whole wedding and was exhausted. Most of the guests had left by this point. "I've got to go," Mom said to me in tears. "Can you stay here and tidy up? Take down the flowers and stuff." The few remaining guests helped us dismantle the garlands that were wrapped around the railing. All of a sudden, the floral sprays from the wedding became flowers for a funeral.

* * *

We held a party for Mom and Dad's fiftieth wedding anniversary at Sandy's house in Leaside.

It was a beautiful October afternoon, and we set up tables for a sit-down lunch in Sandy's huge backyard. My brother made a speech, as did several guests, and congratulations from the queen and the prime minister were read. We had prepared a play called *This is Your Life* in which we told stories about Mom and Dad's life with the seven grandchildren acting out the roles. Duncan narrated. Sandy's son, Robbie, was six foot two by that point, so he played my dad. My daughter, Leah, who was eight, played my mom. All of the other grandchildren each had a number of roles for different scenes. The guests laughed a lot as we re-enacted the time Mom and Dad's landlord nailed the boots to the floor. At the end, we called Mom and Dad up and did a closing song with everyone joining in. Together, we sang "Love, Oh, Careless Love," but changed the words to 'Love, Oh, Lasting Love.'" People thought the show was great and kept coming up and congratulating us. Mom overheard one guest telling me that she knew I must have written the script.

"You did a great job, Jackie," she said. "I remember you putting on plays at the cottage when you were a child."

Mom interjected. "Yeah, she did a great job because Charlie and I gave her great stories to write about. It wouldn't have been anything without our lives to laugh about."

I felt like I'd been punched in the stomach. No one said anything about Mom's comment.

Everyone went home at around three o'clock in the afternoon, still smiling. The party was a great success.

* * *

After every weekend of partying, Sundays were very quiet. We had a lovely brunch after church, and then Mom prepared a casserole to eat later on TV tables in front of the television. Mom and Dad went for a long nap on Sunday afternoons, and the three of us kids learned to keep ourselves busy. On Sunday nights, Dad watched football or some other sport until it was time for "Lassie" and "Walt Disney," which we all watched together.

I had been a lead in our high school musical and made the mistake one night of singing aloud the lines from one of my songs while sitting on the couch as my dad watched football.

"We'll, it's been a long day," I sang. *"We'll it's been a long, been a long, been a long day."*

"Jackie, cut it," Dad snapped. "The show's over. You're not on stage anymore."

I felt as though I'd been knocked to the ground. After that, the two of us sat in silence.

Following dinner, we tidied up and Mom and Dad went straight to bed at about eight o'clock. The house was dark and spooky on Sunday nights. Dad said he had to go to bed early on Sundays because he had "the yips." Eventually I took that to mean he was hungover and had to get his sleep to be ready for another week of work.

19

Dark Times III

In 1997, my husband, Ivan was a Toronto high school teacher. At that time, Ontario Premier Mike Harris proposed sweeping changes to the province's education system with Bill 160. He promoted charter schools and a new educational funding formula that would drastically limit the freedom of local schools to make their own decisions. Parents and educators all over the province were furious. Teachers across Ontario went on a six-week strike.

The first morning of the strike, my mother called. "Your husband is a criminal," she said. "He's breaking the law by going on strike. Tell him to go back and teach."

"He's not a criminal. It's a legal strike. Every teacher in the province is on the picket line today."

"Well, tell him I'm ashamed of him," said Mom.

"I've got to go, Mom," I said and hung up the phone. I stood there shaking, staring out the window until my vision cleared.

I told Ivan about the conversation with my mother when I saw him that night.

"She was so obnoxious," I said. "As if you would cross the picket line and be the only scab in the province. Your fellow teachers would never speak to you again."

"That's not the point," said Ivan. "This is an important strike. What the government wants is disgusting. They're just trying to dismantle our public education system."

"Oh, I agree," I said.

"Besides, what do you expect from your mother? She's as right-wing as they come."

As co-founder of the East End Parents' Network I was due at Queen's Park for a protest on the first day of the strike. We'd met with parent groups from across the province and planned to take our children into the legislature and let the MPPs babysit them. I took Eliana who was eight, Leah who was five, and Victor who was only five months old. We joined hundreds of parents inside the building where children were running everywhere. I had a copy of Bill 160 with sticky notes on the pages I wanted to discuss with the Minister of Education, David Johnson. He was scheduled to hold a press conference, but when he heard there were parents in the building, he cancelled. Most of the parents left.

Along with some other parents, I went up to visit our NDP MPP, Frances Lankin. I had Eliana and Victor with me. Leah had gone out with another parent for some ice cream. While visiting with Frances, we made placards for later.

After a while, Frances told me David Johnson had rescheduled his press conference. I decided to attend with Eliana and Victor and another parent. We couldn't get into the media room, so we waited outside. The other parent held Victor's stroller and I stood with Eliana.

What happened next is still a blur. As Johnson stepped out of the media room, I approached him with Eliana at my side. "Mr. Johnson," I said, "I'm a parent, and I'd like to ask you a few questions about Bill 160." Immediately, security guards surrounded me and separated me from Eliana. Johnson ignored us totally, stepped into an elevator and disappeared.

The media surrounded Eliana and me in our separate corners. I could hear her screaming, "They're taking away my mommy."

Reporters shoved their microphones in her face and asked her, "What do you think of your mother bringing you down to Queen's Park like this?" Cameramen shone their lights on her and filmed her as she cried.

Other reporters filmed me being pulled away by security guards. "Why would you bring your daughter to Queen's Park?" they asked in disgust. For about ten minutes, security guards pushed and pulled me in front of the cameras, while reporters continued to grill both Eliana and me. Kathleen Wynne, who later became Ontario's Premier, was there that day as a member of a parent group. She stood by and watched.

When it was all over, Eliana and I took our bruised bodies and souls back up to Frances Lankin's office. Frances felt so badly that she gave Eliana one of her favourite dolls she had been given when she was Minister of Health in the NDP Government. She turned on the television, and there we were - plastered all over the six o'clock news.

Poor Ivan didn't even know we had gone to Queen's Park that day. He turned on the television and changed from station to station. He saw his wife and daughter being harassed on every channel. When I called him and explained, he said it reminded him of the police in Chile after the coup. Eventually, I met up with the parent who had taken Leah for ice cream and we all drove home.

At home, we had calls from so many friends asking if we were all right. Eliana's principal and our minister even called to check on us. Eliana and I were so traumatized by the event that we didn't leave the house for three days. I lay awake, nursing my bruised arm. Eliana woke up with nightmares for weeks.

The day after the protest, my mother called. She was livid. "Do you know what you've done to my reputation?" she demanded. "I could barely walk through the halls of the Granite Club this morning without people asking about you." I paced back and forth across the kitchen floor as she continued. "I saw you on TV last night, and it was disgusting. I expect an apology."

"I didn't do anything wrong," I said, "and even if I did, I certainly don't owe you an apology for anything. This had nothing to do with you."

"Well, I won't be speaking to you until I get an apology," she said. "You've humiliated me in front of my friends."

"Like I said, don't hold your breath."

"You're not welcome in this house until you say sorry."

"Is that it?" I asked, "Because I have to go now." I hung up the phone. I sat down and put both hands over my face. Within seconds, they were warm with tear. Even if she was mad at me, did she really have no concern for her granddaughter, that little girl crying and calling out for her mom?

Weeks went by and our life got back to normal - minus the contact with my parents. Then, my dad came over. He was always the peacemaker. Dressed in his overcoat and fedora, he stood in the living room, while I sat on the couch. "Jackie, I want you to come to my seventieth birthday party," he said, "but Mom needs an apology. Can't you just say sorry and get it over with?"

"I don't owe her anything," I said. "If I would apologize to anyone it would be Eliana, and I've done that, believe me."

We didn't go to my dad's seventieth birthday party. We missed Christmas, too. One day, in the early spring, I was sitting having lunch with the kids when my mother burst through the door with a plant and some oranges. She threw them into the front hallway and left. Oranges rolled across the living room floor. Eliana, who was having trouble learning how to read, said, "I think Granny's mad at me because I can't read."

Leah, age five said, "No, she's just mean."

"Eli," I said, shaking, "Leah's right. Granny's behaviour has nothing to do with anyone but me."

Months went by and Mom and I still didn't speak. My father dropped in from time to time trying to get me to apologize. I refused.

Finally, one afternoon in October, after my parents had missed Victor's first birthday and most of his first year of life, I sat down with Ivan at the kitchen table.

"I can't take it anymore," I said. "Life is too short. Will you come with me to my parents' house today to see if we can put this thing behind us?"

"Are you going to apologize?" asked Ivan.

"No, I'm not. But it's gone on too long."

"Well, we better go before they get into their martinis, or it'll be a big waste of time."

We drove there together. I knocked on the door at about four-thirty that Saturday afternoon. Mom's face went blank when she opened the door.

"Can we come in?" I asked. "We'd like to talk."

"Okay."

They offered us a drink, but we refused. "Why don't you hold off on your martinis, too, until we've had a chance to talk," I said.

We gathered down in the family room. I sat in a chair across from my father, who was in his regular spot across from the TV. Mom sat beside him in her chair. Ivan was on the couch. The late afternoon sun shone on the large pine coffee table in the middle of the room.

"I love you both very much, and I miss you," I said. "But I'm not here to apologize. I want to tell you about what happened at Queen's Park that day, so you understand."

I told my parents that we were at Queen's Park with hundreds of other parents and children as a day of action.

"Oh, I didn't know that." Mom rubbed her hands together nervously. "I thought you took Eliana and went there alone."

I explained how the security guards pulled Eliana and me apart and how the media surrounded us in a scrum.

She leaned forward in her chair. "It must have been very frightening."

"Yes, it was terrifying, and it haunts both Eliana and me to this day," I said. "And it's only been made worse by not having our family around for support. I was so hurt when Victor turned one and you missed his birthday."

"It's been a long year," said Ivan.

"Well, let's put it behind us now and get together as soon as possible," said Mom.

Dad fiddled awkwardly with the TV converter. "Well, I for one am sorry about the whole thing."

* * *

While Mom and Dad were still alive, we had a family tradition of going to the Granite Club for Easter brunch after church. Duncan, Sandy, and I would join my parents with our spouses and our children.

One year, when Eliana was about sixteen, we had a private dining room with our own waitress and bartender.

Dad was not in a good mood.

"Diane, I told you, I don't like olives in my martini," Dad said to the bartender. "Get me another one, *now*."

Diane came back with a martini on ice in a lowball glass. She was a small woman with black hair and was dressed in her waitressing garb. "That's more like it. Didn't you go to bartending school?"

"Yes, sir, I did," she answered.

"Yes, Mr. Cane. You address me as Mr. Cane."

"Yes, Mr. Cane."

About fifteen minutes went by and Diane was busy getting everyone drinks. My father raised a finger, as she rushed past with a full tray. "Diane, another martini for Mrs. Cane and me."

"Yes, sir," said Diane.

"Yes, who? What did you call me?"

"I'm sorry. Yes, Mr. Cane," she said.

"What's my name?"

"Mr. Cane."

"And don't you forget it."

As Diane stepped out of the room to get the drinks, Eliana talked with her cousins, Annie and Katy. "I'm so embarrassed by Grandpa's behaviour."

"I know," said Annie pushing back her long blonde hair. "He's being so rude."

"He's always like that," said Katy, as she put butter on her roll. "He's a grump."

Diane came back with the martinis.

"Here you go, Mr. Cane."

"That's more like it," Dad said.

Diane left the room to get some Bloody Caesars for the other adults.

"Diane!" my father barked. "Diane, get in here."

"Yes, Mr. Cane? What do you need?" She was taking short, shallow breaths by this time.

"Why did you leave the room?" Dad asked.

"I was getting some drinks."

"Well, I'm going to need some wine in a minute, so don't go far," he said.

"No, no." said Diane. "I'll be right back."

"Tom, give the poor girl a break," Mom said from the other end of the table.

"Dad, she's working really hard," I said. "You're making her really nervous."

"I don't care how nervous I'm making her," he said. "I'm paying for top service."

After Dad kept harassing Diane, Eliana got up and went to the bar. She told me later what she said: "Diane, I just want to say sorry for my grandfather's behaviour. He's embarrassing all of us. We think you're doing a wonderful job, and you certainly don't deserve to be treated this way. Please accept our apology."

"Oh, thank you," said Diane. "I appreciate you taking the time to say that."

Dad wasn't always as bad as he was that Easter, but he could be a real tyrant in restaurants and at special family dinners. I often felt like he was holding the entire family hostage.

* * *

Years went by and Mom and Dad were in their eighties and living at their condo. We convinced them both to get Lifelines, which they wore around their necks.

One night, after several martinis, Dad fell while using his walker to move from the den to his bedroom. When the Lifeline alarm sounded, the medical alert company called Sandy.

"Is this Sandy Cowan?"

"Yes, it is."

"We're calling to let you know your father has had a fall."

"Again?" asked Sandy. "Is he okay?"

"As far as we know, he's fine. You'll have to follow up."

Sandy contacted the concierge at Mom and Dad's condo and he went up and put my father to bed - again.

Sandy called Mom the next morning. "So, Mom, Dad fell again. I got a call from Medical Alert last night. You've got to cut back on the martinis."

"Oh, that's not the problem, honey. Dad just loses his balance."

"Well, the martinis don't help. Maybe you need more care. We could ask Bailey to stay later than five in the evening."

"We're not doing that. I'll deal with the problem."

Mom "dealt with the problem" by cancelling the contract with Medical Alert and not telling us. They kept wearing the Lifelines.

One night, a few weeks later, when they were drinking their martinis and having their dinner on TV tables in the den, Dad decided he was going to bed. As he started making his way towards the bedroom, his walker slipped out from under him. He fell to

Mom and Dad's Martinis

the floor and passed out. Mom stumbled over to him and tried to get him up. He didn't budge.

She was a tiny, frail woman by that stage, and she was very drunk. She didn't want to call the concierge because she knew we would find out, so she decided to leave him lying on the dining room floor and went to bed.

Bailey came in the next morning at eight and found Dad where Mom had left him. Bailey was able to get him up and helped him get a hold of his walker and go to bed. Then she called Sandy, and Sandy called Duncan and me.

"She left him there, Jackie," Sandy said. "All night."

I closed my eyes. I felt dizzy with despair.

Sandy and I decided to visit my parents the next day to talk about the incident. Mom hadn't been going out much because she was having terrible stomach problems. Dad was always home.

Sandy and I arrived promptly at ten the next morning. Mom was still in her nightgown and housecoat, and Dad was dressed in grey flannel pants, a plaid shirt, and his favorite yellow cashmere cardigan. It was very rare to see my mother in her pyjamas at that time of day - an indicator of how sick she was feeling. The four of us gathered around the kitchen table. Bailey left us and went into the den.

"Would you like some coffee?" Mom asked.

"No, I'm fine," I said.

"Me, too," said Sandy. She took a breath. "We're here to talk about what happened the other night, Mom. You know you both mean the world to us. I literally felt sick to my stomach when Bailey called and said she found Dad lying on the floor. The poor woman. She thought he was dead."

At that, tears started running down my cheeks. I could barely handle the shame I felt coming from both my parents.

Sandy continued. "Honestly, I don't think you can go any lower than this." She started to cry. "Dad fell, and you didn't get any help."

"I couldn't lift him," said Mom.

"That's exactly why you need to cut back on the drinking," I said. "When you're both drunk - and don't tell me you weren't - accidents happen. Dad, you can't use your walker properly when you drink. You could break your hip or worse."

"I'm sorry," said Dad. "We didn't mean to bother you."

"You're not bothering us," said Sandy through her tears. "It's because we love you that we're here. We're worried about you."

"Duncan's worried too," I said.

"I'm taking all your gin and vermouth with me today," said Sandy.

Mom burst into tears. "Please don't. I'm an old lady who's sick. All I have left are my martinis."

"It's all *we* have left," added Dad.

I started to sob. "Don't say that. We love you both so much. We want you both to be safe."

"I know you do," said Mom through her tears. I could hardly stand to see her look so vulnerable.

"You know we love you all," said Dad, as he shifted in his chair.

"Then show it," I said. "Take care of yourselves." I hugged both of my parents.

Meanwhile, Sandy went into the den and hid the gin and vermouth bottles behind the couch. "Bailey, I'm putting these bottles back here. Don't tell them. We don't want them drinking anymore."

"I leave at five," said Bailey. "I can't control what they do after that."

"Don't buy anymore alcohol," Sandy said to Mom and Dad.

"Don't do this to me." Mom sat there looking so small and thin. Her hair hadn't been washed in days, and it was matted against her cheeks. "It's all I have to look forward to."

Dad remained seated at the kitchen table and didn't come out to the hallway to say good-bye.

"We love you both so much," I said, as I opened the door to leave. "You've got to be careful. Dad could've died on that floor."

"We're sorry!" Mom cried, as Sandy and I left.

20

The Healing

I am allergic to wine.
But I once tried the old '39.
Besides getting smashed,
I broke out in a rash,
So now gin and tonic does fine.

That's my favourite of eight limericks I wrote for an assignment in grade six. Every one of them dealt with alcohol.

The first time I got drunk was on New Year's Eve when I was fourteen. My parents were at a party, so Duncan and I helped ourselves to the fully stocked bar, adding water to the bottles so they looked full. It was fun at the time.

"Duncan, pour in a little rum," I said. "They're not big rum drinkers, so they won't miss that."

"Okay." He poured a bit of rum into the pitcher. "And how about some rye?"

"Yeah, that's good. What about a bit of gin?"

"No way," said Duncan. "They know their gin like the back of their hand. Here's some bourbon. That hardly ever gets touched."

A year later, my friend Stephanie Mortimer and I raided my parents' liquor cabinet one night when my parents were out. We took a bottle that was almost empty and added a little bit from several bottles until it was full. Then we went out in a field and drank the entire bottle. We sat on our jackets because the ground was cold. I plugged my nose as I took swigs of the gross mixture. Tall grasses surrounded us and rubbed against our cheeks. Stephanie was petite. She got so drunk that she passed out in the middle of a road while we were walking to a party. A man in a station wagon drove by and picked us up. He was an elderly gentleman wearing horn-rimmed glasses. He laid Stephanie in the back seat, and I sat beside her. I gave him the address of the party. "Can you drive us to 49 Burdock Road? That's where Stephanie lives." Out cold in the back seat, Stephanie started foaming at the mouth.

The man looked back and saw the foam. "Your friend is very sick. I'm taking her to the hospital." He turned the car around and headed for North York General.

"No, please. Just take her home," I begged. "She'll be fine."

The man sped to the Emergency entrance, made sure she was safely in the hospital and drove off. Stephanie lay there with white bubbles oozing out of her mouth. My heart started racing, and I could hardly breathe. A doctor came out to talk to me.

"Can you tell me what your friend has injected, inhaled or ingested?" He ran a hand through his grey hair.

I pictured the look on my mother's face. "She hasn't had anything that I know of. We were just on our way to a party, and she passed out on the road."

"Come on, now," he said. "Tell me the truth."

"Like I said. She's had nothing that I know of," I said, feeling sick to my stomach.

I waited and waited. The doctor came out again.

"I know your friend has had something. You'd be helping us a lot if you could shed some light on the situation, so we can help her."

This time, I flashed on my father, and the look he got when he had three or more drinks, and I answered back at him. "I'm telling you, I don't know anything." Finally, the doctor called me into the room where Stephanie lay motionless.

"You stand by her feet," he said. "Now tickle her foot with your fingers."

I did as he asked.

"See how she doesn't react? She's totally unresponsive. Your friend is very, very ill. I think she has severe alcohol poisoning. We're admitting her to hospital. Tell me what she had."

"I told you. I don't know."

"At least give us her phone number so we can call her family," said the doctor.

I felt like I was going to vomit. I did as they asked.

Stephanie's parents came and started asking me the same questions. Her mother was small like Stephanie. "What did Stephie take, Jacelyn?" She looked drawn.

"As far as I know, she didn't have anything. She must have had something before she came to my house."

"That's not possible." Her father looked uncomfortable in his overcoat and bifocals. "I dropped her off at your house this evening, and she was fine."

"Well, I don't know." My head was pounding.

Stephanie was in the hospital for a week.

One night while I lay staring at the ceiling, the phone rang. Dad answered from his bedroom where both he and Mom were in bed. My heart hammering, I listened at my bedroom door.

"Yes, hello Mr. Mortimer. What? That's terrible. She did? I'm so sorry. Oh, we will. You can count on it. Is there anything we can do for Stephanie? Yes, yes, of course. Thank you. Good night." He hung up the phone. "Jacelyn, get in here."

Stephanie had regained consciousness and had told her parents the whole story.

"This is disgusting," said my mother. "That girl almost died."

"Where did you get the alcohol?" asked my father, sitting on the edge of his bed.

I stared at my bare feet. "I took it from your liquor cabinet."

"How dare you," said Mom. "That's not yours to take."

"Never mind that," said Dad. "You're fifteen - *FIFTEEN!* The drinking age is twenty-one! You broke the law!"

"And you broke our trust," said my mother. "You also broke the trust of that poor girl and her family."

"We're going to have to put a lock on the liquor cabinet," my father said. "And you're grounded for two months."

"And while you're grounded, I want you to read the Bible, cover to cover," said Mom. "You obviously need to learn the difference between right and wrong."

I thought it was a fair punishment although I didn't do the reading. It was also impossible for my parents to hold me accountable for the grounding because they were out so often. They never did put a lock on the liquor cabinet.

* * *

As our kids grew up, I started drinking a few glasses of wine with dinner. By the time I was in my mid-forties, I'd added a couple of Bloody Caesars before dinner.

"Dinner's ready, Jackie," said Ivan one night. "Call the kids."

"Let me just finish my Caesar," I said.

"Honey, dinner's gonna get cold," he said. "Eli, Leah - dinner."

I put my drink on the table and poured myself some wine. "How was school today, girls?"

"It was great," said Eliana. "We had drama. I loved it."

"Ms. Stitt did drama? That's fantastic," said Ivan.

We talked some more, and I poured myself another glass of wine. "How about you Leah, how was kindergarten?"

"I painted a big flower with a sun," she said. "I'm going to bring it home when it's dry."

We continued talking, and I drank a few more glasses of wine. I leaned forward on the table.

"Time for baths. Eliana, I'll be up after I finish the dishes. Help me clear, Eli."

"I'll do that," said Ivan. "I think you should go to bed."

"No, no, I can do the dishes." Clumsily, I dropped some plates in the sink.

"Stop, Jackie." Ivan put his hand on top of mine. "You're going to break things. Go to bed."

The girls were watching me as I stumbled upstairs.

"I think you need to see someone about your drinking," Ivan said, as we lay in bed that night. "You're drunk every night at dinner, and it's not good for the kids. It's not good for anyone: certainly not you."

I ignored his suggestion for a while, but he insisted. I wasn't feeling good about myself or my drinking. Eventually I took him up on it and found a wonderful therapist named Penny Watson. She was formerly a medical doctor, but left her practice to specialize in individual, couple, and family therapy.

I went to my first appointment at her grand home in the Beaches neighbourhood in Toronto. My stomach was filled with butterflies as I arrived. Just seeing the front door of her house made me feel better. It was cornflower blue. I let myself in as Penny had instructed. The walls inside were painted the same colour, and it was very soothing. She had photographs of her children on the walls. There was a large book with a thought for the day on the front hall table. I sat down on a chair in the hallway and waited. Soon, a door opened and out came another client followed by Penny. She had light-blonde hair and was dressed in black leggings and a long black top. She had beautiful silver bangles on her wrists with matching earrings.

"You must be Jacelyn. Come on in." She pointed to a large blue comfy chair and I sat down. When she went into the kitchen to get us some coffee, I sized up the room. Penny's chair matched mine. There was a grand piano in the corner, a magnificent Persian rug on the floor, and interesting art on the wall. A framed doll's dress really piqued my curiosity.

She returned with the coffee and sat across from me. "Have you ever been in therapy before, Jacelyn?"

"Yes, once when I was twenty-four, I was hospitalized for being suicidal and having anorexia. I did therapy while I was there. It changed my life."

"How so?"

"Well, I learned that I had really low self-esteem and had been scapegoated as a child. I realized I needed to be kinder to myself. I eventually quit my job in media production and drove out West to find a job with a newspaper. I stopped in at the Winnipeg Tribune and they gave me an assignment to see if I could write. I took the completed piece back to the editor, and he gave me a job. Then, I moved to Winnipeg."

"Your parents must have been proud of you."

"Not my mother. When I called to tell her, she started talking about how she used to do some writing for the *Varsity* at U of T."

"Is that a pattern in your relationship - sorry, is she still alive?"

"Absolutely. It's all about her."

"Can you give me some other examples?"

"Well, when I was twenty-eight, my future husband Ivan and I decided to move in together. I knew my mother wasn't going to be happy about it, so I went to my minister and talked with her. She asked me if I loved him and I said, 'Yes.' She told me that everyone deserved a bit of joy in their life. I wanted to become a United Church minister at the time." I looked down at my hands. "My mother had a lot of pull at the church. She met with the same minister and told her that I was a sinner and that they shouldn't consider me as good ministerial material. She told me this and then didn't speak to me for weeks."

"And your father? Where does he come into all of this?"

"He's more of a peacemaker, but he can be very self-centred too."

"Tell me more," Penny said attentively.

"When I was thirty-two, I completed my master's degree in Canadian history," I said. I was the first woman in my family to get any kind of a degree, let alone a master's. My mother started at U of T, but left early to marry my father. I invited them to my M.A. graduation, but they never came. They thought it was a big waste of time."

"Oh, I'm sorry. That must have been a terrible disappointment."

"Yes, it was."

I spent a lot of time that week thinking about my parents. I returned to see Penny again. "Tell me a bit more about your relationship with your parents."

"I've had some of the best times in my life with them. They love to party. And the wonderful music my dad brought into the house. For that, I feel so lucky. But, on the other hand, they're both pretty caught up in their own world."

"Can you say more about that?"

"Well, neither of them has ever once asked Ivan about his family in Chile - even after he came back from his brother's funeral." I paused. "Years ago, I invited them both to come with Ivan and me to see a screening of the movie 'Missing' about the military coup in Chile. I thought it would help them to understand what Ivan had gone through. Believe it or not, my mother said that they wouldn't waste their time seeing some dumb movie about Chile."

"That must be really upsetting for you."

"Yes, it is. I feel badly for him. It's like he's invisible. Our kids notice it too."

Penny looked at me and nodded. "Sounds like that's painful for all of you."

It took months of weekly visits before I cried.

"I remember a horrible night," I told Penny that afternoon. "My dad was so angry at me for something - I don't remember. I was only eighteen. I was standing in the family room. Mom and Dad were sitting down having their martinis. We were arguing about something. My dad jumped out of his chair and ran towards me. He put both hands around my neck and started choking me. He was so strong. I don't know what would have happened if my mother hadn't been there."

My face was flush with tears. I couldn't stop. I was crying about Dad trying to strangle me. I was crying about him ripping up my drawing. I was crying about Mom dropping me off at the doctor's in her tennis togs when I was suicidal. I returned session after session and released a torrent of tears.

Penny provided me with a caring and safe space to deal with my pain. She was patient when necessary and pushed when it helped. At one appointment I recalled an incident at a rental cottage on Georgian Bay. "I was ten years old," I said. "Sandy and I were sharing a bedroom. Mom and Dad were hosting a gambling party for about twenty of their friends. Our bedroom was next to the bathroom. Sandy was asleep when I heard Mom go into the bathroom and sit on the toilet. She got up and fell over. I could hear her laughing. Then I heard Jim Baldwin go in."

"'Dot, baby,' he asked, 'what are you doing on the floor with your pants down?' He started to laugh. 'Let me help you,' he said. He told my mom to get up. Then he continued, 'Let me pull your underwear up. Stand still.' They were both in hysterics. I think I remember his exact words: 'Let's pull your pants up. Can you do them up? Here Dottie. Stay still. There you go, baby. Now get outta here and let me pee.'" I was crying again.

"How did that make you feel?" asked Penny.

"I was so ashamed of my mother," I said through my tears. "I felt horrified and humiliated at the same time."

Penny nodded. "Anything else?"

I looked at her. "I was so frightened."

* * *

Talking about my parents all the time was very challenging. I was making good progress in therapy, but was still struggling with my drinking. As the years went by, I found that I had bouts of severe depression, anxiety, and unmanageable mood swings. One Sunday night, when Ivan was at the library, I was home with the kids. Eliana was fourteen, Leah was eleven, and Victor was six. I had been drinking. I was in my pyjamas and took one of Ivan's belts into the bathroom. Eliana had seen me lying on my bed crying earlier. As I looped the belt over the rod and began to put it around my neck, she knocked at the door.

"Mom, what are you doing? You've been in there a long time."

"Just leave me alone, Eliana. I'm busy."

Eliana got a dime and pried open the lock. She found me with the belt around the rod. She immediately ran to the phone and dialed 911. "My mother is trying to kill herself, and I'm home alone with my younger sister and brother."

Within minutes the police came, followed by an ambulance. I was sitting in a heap on the bathroom floor crying. "I'm so sorry, kids. I'm so sorry."

One police officer looked around at all the framed children's art on the wall and said, "It looks like this house is filled with love." They were very gentle with me.

Just then, Ivan walked up the stairs in shock. "What's going on here? I was at the library and had a sense I needed to come home. Where are you taking her?"

"Mom was trying to kill herself," Eliana said.

"Oh my God. Why'd you do that, Jackie?"

"We're taking her to Toronto East General," said one of the paramedics. "Come on, Jacelyn. Let's help you into the ambulance."

"She's going to be okay, kids," Ivan said. "We'll go see her tomorrow. Come on, let's go downstairs."

"I don't want to go," I said. "I'm sorry. I'm so sorry."

"It's okay, Mom," said Eliana. "It's the best place for you to be." She hugged me and started to cry. "We'll see you tomorrow."

Ivan and the kids came to see me the next day. "I'm sorry I called the police and the ambulance, Mom," said Eliana. "I was just so terrified." She held my hand and sat on the bed.

"No, honey. *I'm* sorry. I don't know what I was thinking. Everything's going to be okay."

"When can you come home?" asked Leah. She sat on the other side of the bed. Victor lay his head down by my head, but said nothing.

"I'm not sure, but I think soon," I said.

Ivan stood at the end of bed and looked very anxious.

I was in the hospital for ten days. While there, I was diagnosed with bipolar disorder which helped to explain so much of my behaviour, my depression, my anxiety, and the mood swings I had experienced for so long. They gave me anti-depressants and anti-anxiety medication along with mood stabilizers. Soon, I began to feel so much better. The staff members at the hospital connected me with Lou Kant, a local psychiatrist. They also instructed me to see my therapist regularly.

That week at Penny's, I told her everything. "Why do you think you did that?" she asked.

"Well, first of all, I was drunk. Secondly, I was extremely depressed. I was also suffering from those horrible mood swings. As I've mentioned to you before, at one point, I would feel absolute euphoria and days later, I'd be in the depths of despair."

"Well, I'm glad you now have the bipolar diagnosis. It's treatable with the right medications and ongoing therapy. We've talked about how alcohol is a depressant," she said. "Also, people with bipolar often have comorbid alcoholism. The two often coexist. These factors could have triggered your drinking that night."

"Interesting," I said. "I didn't realize that."

"As I've mentioned in the past," said Penny, "with two alcoholic parents, your chances of being an alcoholic are very high. Add the confirmation of bipolar to the mix and the probability of having a drinking problem is extremely likely. If you're ready for it, we may need to talk about you becoming part of a program that helps people deal with their drinking."

"Yeah, I guess so."

"I think that's a huge step, Jacelyn." Penny picked up her pad and pen to take some notes.

"Tell me again why you think your parents drink?"

"Well, my mom's mother died when she was fourteen and my grandfather remarried within months. Mom was never allowed to grieve the death of her mother. I think that's had a huge impact on her ability to express emotion."

She nodded, taking notes. "And your father?"

"It's not so clear with my dad. He had a happy childhood, I think. I know my grandfather suffered from depression." I paused. "Honestly, now that I think of it, Dad might suffer from bipolar as well. He'll get incredibly agitated so quickly and be calm ten minutes later. He loses his cool over the smallest thing. He'll scream and yell if his TV isn't on the right channel. He freaks out when a light bulb burns out. Hours later he'll be the life of the party."

"That sounds like he could have bipolar. There's a lot of research that indicates it's a genetic disorder." She leaned towards me. "How's your immediate family dealing with your suicide attempt? How are the kids?"

"I'm really worried about them. I've apologized a thousand times, but they're all really traumatized."

"May I suggest that you see a family therapist? I know a very good one. Her name is Martha Howard. I trained with her in Italy. You'll like her, and I think it would help the family process the trauma."

I got Martha Howard's number and set up an appointment for the whole family. Martha's office was soothing, full of knick-knacks that had to do with children and families. There was a doll made of cloth on the coffee table and an Inukshuk on the window sill. A basket of small toys lay on the floor near the front door. We sat in comfortable chairs around Martha, a cheery woman with short brown hair. After the introductions, she said. "So, tell me what brings you here today."

There was silence for a minute. I started. "Well, I tried to commit suicide three weeks ago and my kids where in the house. Ivan came home after. I was in the hospital for ten days."

"That must have been very scary for you," Martha said to Eliana.

"It was - and I was the one who called 911. I feel badly that I did that."

"But, you were only trying to help," said Martha. "You were being the responsible oldest child."

"I suppose so," said Eliana "but I still feel awful about it."

"I think it's natural for you to have negative feelings about it," said Martha. "It must have been horrible to witness. What about you, Leah?"

"I feel terrified and sad for my mom," she said. "She didn't want to go to the hospital. I still have nightmares about the police bursting in our front door and taking Mom away in an ambulance. I'm afraid it could happen again."

"It won't happen again, Leah," I said.

"Let's just stick with Leah's feelings for a minute," Martha said to me. "Leah, your parents have taken a great step by bringing all of you here today. That is a huge step on the road to healing."

"I know, I know," Leah said, looking at me and smiling.

"And what about you, Victor?" Martha asked.

Little Victor got up and went and sat on the floor in the corner. He began playing with a Slinky. He never said a word.

"Victor, are you okay?" I asked him. Not a word. I got up and sat beside him on the floor. "Honey, how are you feeling?" I stroked his hair gently.

He pulled away from me and said nothing. He tossed the Slinky back and forth from hand to hand. I stayed seated beside him, knowing that I had caused his pain and would also need to be there for his healing.

"And Ivan," said Martha, "what about you?"

"I'm upset that Jackie was drunk. I don't think she would have done this without the drinking. It's a problem."

"Can we get back to that?" asked Martha. "I just want to stick with the feelings for now."

"Okay, I'm worried," said Ivan.

Eliana looked at her knees. "I'm afraid."

"Me too - and sad." Leah moved forward in her chair looking forlorn.

"I feel so guilty," I said. "I feel so badly."

"I know you do, Jacelyn, but right now I want to focus on what's going on with the others," said Martha.

I nodded, feeling sick to my stomach.

We talked more and made an appointment to return the following week.

"Last week, you mentioned alcohol as a problem. Can we talk about that a bit today?" asked Martha.

My mouth went dry.

"There's no question Mom drinks too much, said Eliana. "She's often drunk by the end of dinner. It makes me really nervous."

Sorry, mom, but Eli's right," said Leah. "It's become a lot worse this year."

Victor was back in the corner playing with the Slinky.

"Jackie's parents are both huge drinkers," said Ivan. "They've been drinking four or five huge martinis a night since I met them. And, as we said last week, Jackie's just been diagnosed with bipolar disorder. We think her father has it, too. Drinking and bipolar often go together." Ivan crossed his legs and thought for a moment. "But her parents' drinking has been with Jackie all of her life. It's affected our kids – all of us."

"I can't call my mother after seven at night because she'll be drunk."

"That must be difficult to be around," said Martha.

"We don't see them too often," I said.

"It sounds like there's a drinking problem," said Martha. "Why not commit to making this the last generation with a problem? Jacelyn, Alcoholics Anonymous has helped so many people I know. They couldn't have done it without it."

"I've tried A.A. a few times, and I didn't like it. It bothers me the way people have to stand up, say their name and say, 'I'm an alcoholic.' I'm not sure I am."

Ivan laughed. "Yeah, right."

I glanced at him and continued. "I'm opposed to A.A.'s twelve-step program. It's not based on one ounce of research. I've heard of a program at the Jean Tweed Centre which focuses on women and substance abuse," I said. "I'll check that out."

"That would be great, Mom," said Eliana. "We'd all support you."

We saw Martha Howard many more times and she helped us immensely.

At one very significant session, she said, "I can really feel the love in this family. You're going to get through this."

* * *

In preparation for the program at the Jean Tweed Centre, Penny recommended that I take an eight-week course in mindfulness meditation. It was based on the incredible work by Jon Kabat-Zinn, an American professor emeritus in medicine and creator of the Stress Reduction Clinic and Centre for Mindfulness at the University of Massachusetts Medical School. The program consisted of eight three-hour weekly sessions in which the participants learned how to meditate, as well as a final six-hour meditation. I was also required to meditate for an hour each day of the eight-week program. To this day, these techniques help me to live in the present moment and to be mindful of what is going on in the present - not the past or the future.

Mom and Dad's Martinis

I agreed with Penny that I would sign up for the three-week intensive day program at the Jean Tweed Centre. It involved individual counselling, group therapy sessions, educational programs, wellness activities, and more.

I entered my counsellor's office. There was a vibrant Latin American rug on the floor and a few feminist posters on the wall.

"What's important to focus on," said my counsellor, Mayla, "is the pain that weaves its way through the addiction." Wearing a poncho and sitting cross-legged in her chair, she was slender with long black hair and wise for someone so young. "And you can't change the pattern of your addiction without changing your life."

"In many ways, I've had a wonderful life. I have a great husband and fantastic children. In that way, I'm very fortunate. And there were many great moments in my childhood as well. I never lacked for anything materially. But, I suffered from a sense of abandonment, neglect, and abuse. I experienced a lot of trauma as a child. I've had a difficult time with my parents who are both alcoholics."

We talked about my parents' drinking and why they drank. "If you can understand their shortcomings, it can help you to forgive them," said Mayla.

"I think I'm reaching a point of forgiveness," I said. "I've been in therapy dealing with these issues for years. I've gained a much better understanding of why my parents behave the way they do."

We talked about whether I considered abstinence or harm reduction as the best option for me. Harm reduction means cutting back on alcohol intake to a safe and healthy limit, but not eliminating it totally. "I think I'd like to try harm reduction," I said. "I'd like to stop drinking daily, but allow myself to have a drink or two when I go out or have a special occasion."

"We fully support harm reduction when it's appropriate," said Mayla. "One strategy is to urge surf. You focus on the present moment – mindfulness - and surf over the urge. Don't give into it. It will pass. We call it H.O.P.E.: Hold On, Pain Ends."

"Hold On, Pain Ends," I said, letting the thought percolate in my brain. "HOPE - I really like that."

I learned wonderful strategies at the Jean Tweed Centre. While there, I watched a "TED Talk" by American researcher, professor, and author Brené Brown, and learned that shame is caused by "secrecy, silence, and judgement. It's lethal," says Brown. "What's needed instead," she notes, "is empathy." She explains the difference between guilt and shame. "Guilt," she says, "tells us that we've made a mistake. We can do something about that. Shame, on the other hand, means 'we are a mistake.'" Brown also talks about the importance of vulnerability and how it is critical if one is going to be innovative, creative, and able to make changes.

At the final group therapy session at the Jean Tweed Centre, eight women sat on chairs in a circle. There was a lit candle in the centre along with a box of Kleenex. I started crying and couldn't stop. "I feel so badly that I've hurt my husband and children so much. I feel so terrible." I had written myself a letter outlining my commitment to my harm reduction strategy, but I knew it wasn't enough. I needed to write to my family, too.

Dear Victor,

I apologize for all the hurt I have caused you with my drinking over the years. I have completed my program at the Jean Tweed Centre and promise to stop drinking regularly at home. I will only have a drink when it's a special occasion or when I go out for dinner. I love you more than anything and am so sorry I've caused you pain. I hope you can accept my commitment to change.

Love,
Mom

I wrote a similar letter to Eliana, Leah, and Ivan. By that time, I had gone one month without drinking anything. It was a new beginning.

Several years have passed and I still attend the Jean Tweed Centre's Continuing Care program weekly. I have benefitted enormously from the staff who lead that program and from sharing experiences with other women in the group who are also dealing with substance abuse issues. While I have had some slips, I have maintained my harm reduction goals for a long time now. I continue to be monitored regularly by my psychiatrist. Together, we assess which medications work best to keep my bipolar stable. As well, I see Penny Watson a few times a month and my family meets with Martha Howard occasionally.

I am also comforted by belonging to Trinity-St. Paul's United Church, a vibrant, progressive, and loving congregation in the heart of downtown Toronto. At every worship service, the minister, Cheri DiNovo, a former NDP MPP in the Ontario Legislature, begins by saying, "Welcome. No matter what you believe, no matter what you don't believe, no matter what you've done, no matter what you've left undone, no matter who you are, no matter who you love, you are welcome here…." Her words are so forgiving and so empowering – they remind me that God is with me – there in every breath I take. And the music, under the direction of Brad Ratzlaff, is always a balm for my soul, allowing me to feel God's love.

I have definitely faced many adversities at the hands of my parents. Nevertheless, I recently sat in the pew at church and watched the sunlight stream through the stained glass window. As I did, I felt so connected to my mother and father. I was filled with gratitude towards them for taking me to church every Sunday as a child and enabling my faith to seep into my pores.

I am so fortunate to have all these supports in my life – and I have worked hard to get where I am today. There is no question, however, that it's my loving family – my immediate family - that is at the centre of all this healing.

At this point, I feel whole. I feel honest. And I feel loved.

21

The Light

Mom died on January 9th, 2015. I went to see Penny a few days after her death.

"You know, I feel a sense of serenity about my relationship with my mother," I said.

"I don't feel angry or bitter. I feel as though, with all the therapy, and with my mother's many illnesses, I've reached a point of forgiveness. It's a kind of acceptance - peace. I loved her. I remember her hugging me and crying with me when my best friend Judy died. It was a beautiful moment."

"That's a wonderful place to be."

Dad died just over a year later. I visited Penny again.

"I feel such a loss. I cried so much at his funeral," I said.

"Well, now they're both gone," said Penny. "That's huge. Your generation is next."

"I suppose," I said. "But, for all my dad's faults, I loved him so much. And I know he loved me. I'm going to miss them terribly. My face was awash with tears. "I remember his music – his wonderful music. It became such a part of me. And I will never forget his jokes. He told the craziest jokes." I laughed and sniffled at the same time.

* * *

It was Thanksgiving, 2016 - the first family gathering without my parents. The entire family was coming to our house for dinner. I asked each person to bring a memory of Mom or Dad or both. It was a mild October day and we were sitting on the deck having cocktails.

"I'll start," I said. "I remember the way Dad taught me to play the ukulele. He taught me with such love. His music had a huge influence on my life."

"I remember when Granny took Mom, Eliana, and me to the Toronto Ladies Golf Club," said Leah. "We ate lunch on the lawn under an umbrella. Granny was dressed in red slacks with a red and white polka-dotted blouse - she looked so classy. She talked about her mother for the first time. I felt so close to her then - she was a real feminist. And I also remember when Granny was near death, and she asked me to paint her nails. That was really important to her. So, I took my nail kit to the Rehab Centre and painted her nails cherry red. There she was with one full leg and half of the other wanting her nails just right. We had a lovely final conversation." She was quiet for a moment. "I remember noticing gangrene under one nail."

Katy, my brother's daughter, held her baby boy, Charlie in one arm and pushed back her brown hair with the other. "Even though Grandpa had a lot of bad days, I remember the first time I took Charlie to meet him. Grandpa couldn't take his eyes off him. He fell in love with him immediately."

"I remember the singalongs with Grandpa," said Katy's sister. She was slight with long blonde hair. "And I loved it when Granny would take all of the women and girls in the family to a show and lunch every Christmas. It taught me to love the arts."

Mom and Dad's Martinis

"I had a very loving relationship with both Charlie and Dot," said Sandy's husband. "There was a mutual respect for many years."

"I have to say, your parents were like peasants with money," said Ivan. "When they drank, they let down their hair and had so much fun."

"Remember when Mom drove Sandy all the way to Barrie in her pyjamas and crashed Dad's car on the way home?" Duncan took a sip of his Bloody Caesar and laughed. "God, what a pair. When Dad coached my hockey team, he got more bench penalties than anyone for yelling at the referee."

"I remember his singsongs," said Victor. "He inspired me to play the guitar."

"Granny was such a strong, independent woman," said Sandy's daughter.

"I loved the way Mom was always willing to try new things," said my brother's wife. "It was amazing that she started playing golf at age sixty-five."

Sandy's son leaned his lanky frame against the railing. "Grandpa came to all my hockey games. He even flew to the states to watch me play on my university team."

"I remember when Leah, Victor, and I performed for Mom and Dad at their retirement party," said Eliana. "It was Grandpa's music that influenced our ability to sing and harmonize like that."

"Mom had an incredible fashion sense," said Sandy, as she modelled one of Mom's capes. "And I'll never forget the way her eyes lit up when I walked in the room." She started to cry. "She was always so happy to see me."

Everyone was close to tears. We were the family now - no more Mom and Dad. But there was a real warmth on the deck that day. And I couldn't help but think, Mom and Dad had so much more than their martinis. They had so much more.

Acknowledgements

Thank you to author Alissa York from Humber College's Creative Writing program whose talent, time, and dedication helped me give birth to this book.

I also give thanks to my husband, Ivan and my children Eliana, Leah, and Victor for continuing to love me through difficult times. I am thankful to them for encouraging me to explore the dark times in our lives and for standing by me during the years of writing this book.

As well, I want to express my love for my parents, Dot and Charlie Cane, whom I miss dearly.

I am also grateful to one of my mom's dearest friends, Joan Beatty and her daughter Sally Beatty, my close friend, who took a trip down memory lane with me. Together, we recalled many of my mom and dad's best moments.

My sister, Sandy Cowan, and my brother, Duncan Cane, were gracious in allowing me to write this book. They also assisted me in remembering the details of these stories.

Thank you to Penny Watson and Martha Howard for helping my family and me through many difficult situations. You both bring such skill, dedication, and compassion to your work.

I am grateful to my psychiatrist, Lou Kant for monitoring my medications all these years and helping me to deal with mental illness.

I have learned so much from Jon Kabat-Zinn and his mindfulness meditation process. I still use his guided meditations regularly – always reminding me to focus on my breath.

I also want to acknowledge the caring staff and other women at the Jean Tweed Centre for encouraging me to make important changes in my living.

As well, I want to express my gratitude to the staff and members of Trinity-St.Paul's United Church who play such an important role in my life.

I am also grateful to the staff members at Kilcoo Camp who gave me permission to use the lyrics to "The Kilcoo Blues", author unknown. Thanks, as well, to Alfred Publishers for granting me permission to print lyrics from Gordon Lightfoot's "If You Could Read My Mind" and to Hal Leonard Publishers for allowing me to print lyrics from "Rose Garden" by Joe South and sung by Lynn Anderson. All other song lyrics used are in the public domain.

And finally, I would be remiss in not thanking the dedicated people at Tellwell Publishing whose blood, sweat, and tears were critical in bringing this book to life.

About the Author

Jacelyn Cane lives in Toronto, Ontario with her husband. She also lives with or near her three children and step-daughter. Jacelyn is a retired primary school teacher who worked with the Toronto District School Board, former Christian educator with the United Church of Canada, and writer. *Mom and Dad's Martinis* is her first book. Please visit Jacelyn Cane.com.

Manufactured by Amazon.ca
Bolton, ON